CAN SOMEONE HELP CARRY MY BAGGAGE?

A Journey from Abuse to Unconditional Love and a Forever Family.

K. A. Cory

ISBN: 1518899021
ISBN 13: 9781518899027
Library of Congress Control Number: 2015918447
CreateSpace Independent Publishing Platform
North Charleston, South Carolina

To my husband, Robert:
Thank you for doing what you do,
as you have said,
so that I could do what was important.

To my children, Ryan, Cassey, and Alex:
Thank you for supporting my late nights helping other children even
though it meant there were a lot less home-cooked meals, game nights, and
undivided attention for you. Thank you for understanding there are a lot
of children who do not have the unconditional love of a parent and that
your mother was called to help them find this love.

To all my families whose names would take up too many pages:
Thank you for stepping up to be the unconditionally loving parents for
your children even if they may not have been the easiest to love. Thank
you for stepping up and helping them carry a little baggage.

CONTENTS

PREFACE

The ruins of a nation begin in the homes of its people.
—Ghanaian proverb

Salvation of a nation is in its families.
—Unknown author

MISSION STATEMENT

I shall ***Leave a Legacy*** by being the World to just one person.

I shall ***Leave a Legacy*** by being a positive influence in the life of just one person.

I shall ***Leave a Legacy*** by shining Christ's love to others through my actions.

I shall ***Leave a Legacy*** by smiling so others might know happiness.

I shall ***Leave a Legacy*** by crying with one person so they will have known someone cared.

I shall ***Leave a Legacy*** by being quiet so that one person will know that someone cared enough to listen.

I shall ***Leave a Legacy*** by being a light in the darkness.

I shall ***Leave a Legacy*** by being a friend to many.

I shall ***Leave a Legacy*** by being an enemy to no one.

I shall ***Leave a Legacy*** by being a hero to one child.

—Katrina Boldin, April 25, 2007

INTRODUCTION

For twenty years my professional career has encompassed various fields of social work. You could say I have actually been in social work my entire life.

As I was growing up, my parents cared for many children who had been forgotten or pushed aside by their biological parents. My parents worked as house parents at Hoosier Boys Town, where they watched over twenty teenage boys. Later on they took teenage foster girls into our home. I grew up watching my parents give to other people's children what many adults do not know how to give to their own children. My parents provided not just food, clothing, and shelter, but also love, attention, and a sense of belonging. All too often children in foster care lose sight of what it means to be loved unconditionally. It is this lack of love and support that prevents any of us from loving others and many times causes us to repeat a cycle of not knowing how to love and provide for our own children. The love and caring we learn as children guide us when we are adults.

I know how to love. I know how to respect others. I know how to show sympathy and empathy. I know how to give back, not just how to live in this world. I know how to do all these things because I have been raised in a family in which love, respect, giving back to others, etc. was common practice. I may not have realized this when I was younger, but concern for others was nurtured within me and is demonstrated by my actions as an adult.

I have worked with children and adults with mental retardation, mental illness, and severe developmental delays. I know how to respect and care for these individuals—not for who the world sees them as, but for how they truly are. They are human beings regardless of whether they fit within society's definition of "normal." Their IQs may be lower than most, the demons in their heads may scream louder than most, but they are deserving and in need of the same love and respect we all need.

I have worked with children in foster care and their biological families, families that many would say are not worthy of respect. These families, regardless of how society views them or my initial impression of them, are loved by the children they have brought into this world. I have seen children who have been beaten, neglected, molested, and forgotten by their biological parents but who nevertheless love these parents. These children know nothing more than what this world has shown them so far. Typically, they do not know that a life without certain kinds of pain is possible: They do not often know there is a world where it is not OK to be touched in ways that hurt. They do not often know that their clothes should be clean and should fit. They do not know they should get food when they are hungry. They do not know that a place to sleep; clothes to wear; food to eat; or freedom from being hit, kicked, or touched should come before their parents' desire to get high, get drunk, or leave for days at a time.

Our children, yours and mine, take for granted that they have a TV to watch, game systems to play, or sports teams to be a part of. These are things that many children assume everyone has, and so our children expect to be provided with all these entertainment sources. However, these HDTVs, PlayStations, and baseball games are luxuries that are not a part of the thinking of a child coming into foster care. A bed not shared with mom's boyfriend, having food when hungry, and not having clothes that are so dirty that the kids at school laugh and point would be good enough for many children starting out in foster care.

Every child should have a chance in life not just to have food, clothing, and shelter; he or she should also have the chance to live, laugh, learn, and become someone amazing. A "forever family" can do just that, as the children in the stories that follow have proven. What matters is not where they started their lives, but the path that their lives have traveled. The children whose lives are discussed in this book have become amazing because of the people they have met, the dreams they have had, and the dreams that ultimately came true, whether through the love of a mom and dad, the love of just a mom, the love of just a dad, the love of two moms, the love of two dads, the love of grandparents, or sometimes the love of a village.

The book uses the term "baggage" referring to the ugly stuff that children (actually all people but used frequently with children in foster care) come with that biological children would not: residual trauma from the abuse and neglect, learning disabilities, mental health, physical aggression, etc. stemming from the abuse and neglect. The book wraps up challenging people to pick up a bag. Give to a child even if you can't adopt.

CHAPTER 1
WHAT DOES A FAMILY LOOK LIKE?

Early in my life, I had the traditional Catholic family unit. I had a mom and dad, neither of whom had never been married previously. My family did not know of divorce, domestic violence, or infidelity. I had heard of people who had been divorced, but I really didn't understand it firsthand. Most of my friends came from families with a mom and a dad. I believed that a mom and dad were the beginning of any family, and that after these two parents, a family included sisters and brothers, with generally a dog or maybe a cat running around. All my cousins came from families that looked a lot like mine. The cousins on my mom's side of the family even had as many siblings as I was used to, at least three or more per family. I myself ended up marrying a man who also had a mom and a dad and three siblings. After all, I grew up thinking this is what a family always looks like. As a child I was able to stretch my idea of "family" minimally, to include families with a mom and dad and only two kids because that was how the families on my dad's side were. His nuclear family still had a mom and a dad who had never been married before, so at least I knew that part was right. Family equals mom, dad, and a couple of kids, or so I believed at an early age.

A few years later in my life, though, my mom and dad decided to care for children who had been abused and neglected, children who had gotten into trouble, and children whom for whatever reason, had no family. After this, my definition of "family" changed from mom, dad, and a few kids (like my own family) to the definition of the "other family," which equaled bad parents and a few kids.

At this point in my life, I really didn't know what those other parents looked like. Mom and Dad just helped the kids. These other families must have each had a mom and a dad as well, but they were not very good at their jobs; therefore, my mom and dad had to take over for them. Basically, "family" still was defined by the same parts: mom, dad, and kids. Now, this definition included good or bad moms and dads plus good or bad kids. We were the good ones, and the other kids my parents helped were the bad ones.

<u>George Peter Murdock, an American anthropologist,</u> also describes the term "family" in this way: "The family is a social group characterized by common residence, economic cooperation, and reproduction. It contains adults of both sexes, at least two of whom maintain a socially approved sexual relationship, and one or more children, own or adopted, of the sexually cohabiting adults" (Murdock, *Social Structure* [1949; reprinted, New York: Free Press, 1965]).

Even when my parents were caring for these other children, they were not really a part of our family. They were foster kids, not my parents' kids. Foster kids already had their own families; therefore, they could not be part of my family. They were a part of that bad family.

Several years later I realized that some families didn't live together. Moms and dads would divorce, and then the kids would be shared between two houses. Sometimes this would mean that there would be a mom and a stepdad in one house and a dad and stepmom in the other house, all sharing one set of kids. Then there were those families who had a new set of kids when a divorcing parent remarried. Now the family was made up of a mom and stepdad with two sets of kids, his and hers. These new families, consisting of divorced spouses who produced another set of children with their new spouses, would be known as binuclear families. Do you see the similarities between nuclear and binuclear families still, though? I still had this idea that the family equation consisted of a mom and dad. I was even willing to recognize that family could be made up of a child who lives with his or her grandparents, but, of course, there are still a mom and a dad in this equation; they just happen to be Grandma and Grandpa. I continued to have a very narrow view of what family looked like.

As an adult, my brother showed me a totally different idea of family. He was neither married nor straight. In my old, closed-minded view of family, these two conditions would have prevented any formation of family. Yes, I knew that children were adopted every day. I knew it on a personal level because I gave a child up for adoption my senior year of high school. Therefore, it was very easy for me to understand that there were couples that couldn't have children, and so they adopted a teenage mother's baby. I hadn't been exposed to the idea of older children being adopted. Even the adopted kids from other countries that I'd seen on TV were still pretty young. My brother and his partner had chosen to look into adopting a child or sibling group from foster care. The number of children looking for a home, a family, is mind-boggling: 127,000 in 1999, a high of 130,000 in 2007, and 127,000 as per the most recent AFCARS report of 2011. (Most of the cited data is from the US Department of Health and Human Services Adoption and Foster Care Analysis and Reporting System [AFCARS], which collects case-level data from the state child welfare agencies and prepares aggregate reports. AFCARS documents the number of children in foster care and their status on the last day of each fiscal year. AFCARS also reports the number and characteristics of foster children adopted throughout the year. AFCARS Report 19, which details fiscal year 2011 data, is the most recent and comprehensive data source available. It is available at http://www.acf.hhs.gov/programs/cbresource/afcars-report-19.)

In 2002 I began working for Children's Services in a rather large southern state. Many states have their own views of family, and though such views may not be as closed-minded as mine was when I was growing up, they are still pretty much understood. Family could be a mom and a dad or possibly just a mom. Occasionally family could be just a dad, but in this southern state, two moms or two dads were not considered a family.

When a child or children in foster care have the rights of their biological parents terminated, they become legally free. An attempt to locate an adoptive family is then made. Many times this is a search for a strong family with a mom and a dad who are considered to be able to provide a "normal" life for a child who has come from a bad starting point. In working to find an adoptive family for my first set of siblings, I realized that a mom and a dad were not the perfect definition of family for the children standing before me. With over 4,041 children waiting to be adopted in the state of Texas alone in January 2015, how is it that an agency would limit itself to one definition of what a family looked like?

As an adult, "family" had taken on a whole new definition for me: family consists of people who love you and are willing to protect you no matter what. This can be a mom and a dad, but not always. Depending on what pain has been inflicted on a child, a family may not have a dad at all. A family may need to be assembled with two moms in order to have that sense of safety and sense of being protected. Some loss in a child's life may hurt so badly that having a mom be part of his or her family would be too much to handle. For this family, just a dad will do fine. In order to figure out what a child's forever family looks like, I first must ask each individual child what he or she sees for his or her future family.

I don't ask the question "Do you want a mom and a dad?" I may get a "yes" response for the plain and simple reason that the child doesn't know what else there is to ask for. Instead I try asking, "When you think of the family that you will keep forever, what do you see? A mom and a dad? Just a mom? Just a dad? Two moms? Two dads? Are they young? Are they old? Are they someone you already know?" That forever family may start at the child's school, church, foster home, or maybe with relatives he or she knew a long time ago. Forever is a long time to love and care for someone. A child must have a voice in what "forever" looks like.

The following chapters will take the reader through the lives of some children. The reader will learn each child's story as told by the child, social worker, and prospective adoptive family. The child may not tell their own story if they are too young or have special needs that prevent them from being able to tell their own story.

CHAPTER 2
ABBY AND EDDIE

My name is Abby, and I have two brothers. One is two years older than me, and one is two years younger than me. We are from a small town in Texas where there is a lot of back roads and wooded areas. It makes it really easy to hide out here. It makes it really hard to find us too. Our house is pretty small, and most would call it a travel trailer, but to us it is the only home we know. Our mom has a lot of friends, mostly guys. They like to have a good time, drink, and use needles. I haven't been able to figure out what is so fun about needles. I remember getting a shot once, and it really hurt. I would think that it would really hurt my mom also but she seems to be really happy afterward. Sometimes she is so happy she forgets that my brothers and I are around. Last week she must have been really, really happy because she left for a few days and we didn't know where she went. We didn't go to school then because we didn't know if we should leave the house or not. When Mommy doesn't drink or use her needles to be happy, she can be pretty mean. The last time she was gone for a few days, she came home and she didn't have anything to drink or any needles at the house; and my big brother got beat up something awful. I was afraid that if we left for school, if she came home and we weren't there, we might all get beat up real good. Joey, my big brother, takes the beatin's most of the time. He tells us to stay behind him and to stay quiet. I remember once that Mommy used the last needle, and her boyfriend got so mad. She tried everything to make him happy. She even let him hit Joey again and again so that he wouldn't be mad anymore. He hit Joey so hard that he looked like he was dead. The way his head hit the table and then the ground, I would have sworn he was dead. He did eventually wake up but never really seemed the same after that.

We went to school a few days later, but there was still bruises left on Joey's face. The school counselor called those people with CPS. Not quite sure what that stands for, but Mommy has always told us not to talk to those people. She says that they steal people's kids and lock them away in really bad, scary places. The lady with one of those CPS cards around her neck tried to talk to Joey. He said he couldn't remember what happened, just that he fell and hit his head on the table. It is sad to say, but as bad as Joey got beat that night, he probably really doesn't remember. He wouldn't say anything even if he did remember because that would just about guarantee another beatin' when we got home. We know that lady will come out to the house, but she will tell Mommy that Joey said he couldn't remember, so we won't get in any trouble. That lady can ask all the questions she wants. We know what to say. Mommy taught us the right things to say: "I don't remember." "I tripped." "The dog leash got tangled around my ankles." That last one may not work anymore since the dog ran away. I will have to ask Mommy for something different to tell that lady.

Mommy has a new boyfriend. This one doesn't like to hit people. Mommy says that he is a lover, not a fighter. Not quite sure what that means. They still drink and use needles together just like mommy and her old boyfriend. I am glad that we do not have to worry about getting hit by this new guy. That is always my biggest fear. Mommy's new boyfriend, I think, is rich. They always have a lot to drink and lots of medicine for the needles. Mommy and her boyfriend are always so happy. Mommy makes these weird sounds sometimes when she is happy and starts acting silly. Her boyfriend seems to really like it. He says that he doesn't hit and that we shouldn't be scared of him.

He decided to show Joey how to be nice to girls. He showed him how he is nice to Mommy and told Joey that he should try and be nice to me. I don't really like it when Joey tries to be nice like Mommy and her boyfriend. I don't think that brothers and sisters are supposed to do things like that. I guess I am wrong; Mommy said it is OK. I figure that if it is right for Joey to be nice to me, then I should be nice to Eddie. Mommy and her boyfriend watched to make sure that I did it right. This didn't work at all. Mommy said that her boyfriend could take me in the back of the trailer and show me how to do it right, if he thought that would help. He said that he would show me what it is like when a guy is really nice to a girl. His private is big, and it hurt so much I screamed. I shouldn't have screamed. This really made him mad. Mommy threw my baby brother in the back and told her boyfriend to try "this one." She said that Eddie never cries, and he needs to be treated nice too. Oh, I wish I hadn't screamed. I am really sure that Eddie doesn't have anywhere for his private to go. Eddie never screamed. I guess he was stronger than me.

I have lost track of what boyfriend Mommy has now. It doesn't seem to matter. If they hit us, we don't cry anymore. If they are nice to us, I don't scream anymore, and Eddie never did. Joey seems a little slow since he hit his head so hard. Kids at school say that he is retarded. The school even put him in a special class. We have all missed so much school that we have to go to special classes, but Joey's is one for retarded kids.

Mommy wasn't home when we got back from school today. There was just this lady with the CPS card around her neck. She said that Mommy wasn't going to be home for a few days and that we would have to go with her. Joey tried to use the words that Mommy told us, but "I don't remember" and "I tripped on the dog leash" don't seem to matter when your mother isn't coming home and the CPS people know. The lady took us to her office, and we sat in a room with a TV and some toys for what seemed like forever. Finally, another lady came and told us that they had a home for us to go to. We drove a very long time and finally arrived at some stranger's house. The people seemed nice, and they took us to separate bedrooms. Joey and Eddie were in one and me in the other. The nice lady with the CPS card around her neck left us there.

It was very scary to be in a strange house all by myself. At least Joey and Eddie had each other. I didn't like being by myself, so I was very quiet and went into the room with my brothers. Joey thought that I needed him to be nice to me, or that the mommy at this house sent me in, since when Mommy would send me into Joey's bed that was what he was supposed to do. I don't cry or say no. I know better—that only gets you hit and hit hard.

The mommy of this house walked into check on us kids. She was really mad to see Joey being nice to me. I don't understand. She started yelling and asking all these questions, a really lot of questions:

"What are you doing?" "How long has this been going on?" "Don't you know this is wrong?" "That is bad; you can't do that to your sister."

The lady with the CPS card around her neck was back the very next morning. She stated that we were going to go talk to some people and that then we would go to a new home. I asked what was wrong with the last one. She couldn't seem to think of a good answer, so she said nothing at all.

We went to this place that looked like a house on the outside. Inside, it kind of still looked like a house, a house with an office in the middle of it. The guy took each of us to this playhouse in the back. I don't know what he asked my brothers, but I will tell you what he asked me lots of stuff:

- Who lives at your house?
- What does your house look like? Draw me a picture of all the rooms.
- Who sleeps where?
- What is this color? Child answers and the interviewer tells them it is a different color and asks if this would be a truth or a lie.
- Point to the arm on this picture, point to the leg, and point to the private part. What is that called?
- BIG QUESTION: Has anyone ever touched your private parts?

What do I say? Mommy always told us what to say when we were asked about bruises, but she never told us anything to say if we were asked if someone had been nice to us. Does this mean that I tell the truth? I did promise this guy that I would tell the truth. Mommy didn't say not to tell when people are nice to you. I doubt that it is going to matter if I tell the truth or not. That lady already took us from our mother, and we are going to a second strange house after this. I guess in a way, we are already in the middle of the scary places and may never be going home any way. I don't even know where my mommy went. Why didn't she say good-bye? Fine, I am just going to tell the truth. I hope that the boys tell the truth also. I don't want them thinking that I am the liar. Maybe I should give them a sign so they know that I already told the truth about us being nice to each other and having other people be nice to us. Maybe.

Telling the truth sure does get you a lot of attention. I didn't re-alize that one kid could have to talk to so many people. I have been taken to doctors that had to look at every part of me—by the way,

NOT FUN. Then there were the other ones that said they were doctors but they never took my temperature or anything. Not sure how they can be a doctor if they don't care about my temperature. They made me play these games and work on problems.

The lady with the card around her neck told the foster mom that I needed to talk to more people once a week and that a meeting was going to be held at school because I was so behind. I guess my mommy didn't know that kids are supposed to go to school every day. Mommy must not have known that kids that are the same age are supposed to be in the same classes together. I think that it is really hard to catch up. Most days I don't bother trying. This must be OK because the foster home that I am at right now doesn't seem to mind when my school grades are really bad.

Today I got a new home. I think I have lost count of how many homes I have lived in. I will give the CPS people a little credit; no one hurts me in these homes. I really don't like changing homes, schools, friends...The worst part is being separated from my brothers. The new lady said that I couldn't be with Joey because he is too nice to me and Eddie. Did I mention that I don't get to see the first lady anymore? We got a new caseworker—actually we have had about seven caseworkers. I guess this is normal, seeing as we have been in foster care for four years now. It hasn't been as bad as Mommy said it would be, but it sure would be nice to stay in one place.

⇒⊹ ⊹⇐

I, the caseworker, was assigned this case with a sibling group of three children. Two of them are actually placed together, but I have been told that the older brother can never be placed with his younger brother and sister. Joey has been identified as sexually acting out, perpetrating on his siblings, and cannot be placed with any children younger than he. Even though the kids cannot be placed together, I am fighting for them to be allowed to visit each other.

The case file has traveled through many caseworkers at this point. It would appear that the rights of the parents were terminated over two years ago, but I do not see any documentation where efforts have been made to locate an adoptive family. My first task with this new case is to talk to the kids. The prior caseworker was not able to tell me what type of family she was trying to recruit for these kids.

I met with the children and foster mother, Ms. Violet, for the first time today. The foster mother wanted to know when the children would be adopted. Since there wasn't any documentation to indicate that recruitment efforts had been done, I asked Ms. Violet, the foster mother, how the prior worker had been looking for families. She indicated that she had no idea. She and the children were just told every month that they would have a family real soon. Ms. Violet wanted to know what that meant. So as to not bad-mouth the case practice of a fellow worker, I just stated I was not clear on what efforts had been made so far, but I was aware of some new approaches that we could try. The foster mother, the children, and I sat and talked for quite a while about what they liked, wanted, and needed in a family. Ms. Violet shared information about the children that she was not sure they would chose to share on their own.

I spent the next few weeks working closely with the adoption specialist in the larger office. She was able to register the children on the state website for adoption recruitment: Texas Adoption Resource Exchange (www.dfps.state.tx.us/adoption_and_foster_care). Once children are listed on the website, locating an adoptive family that meets the child's needs and wishes usually becomes a waiting game. I inquired about other possible activities to locate a family. These children were almost teenagers and considered by many to be "not adoptable." On many occasions people from all walks of life (attorneys, other caseworkers, foster parents, even friends) have told me that I have a Pollyanna-like attitude: I see every child through these perfect rose-colored glasses. Many do not believe there is a family for every child, but I DO! If that family is not found before the child's eighteenth birthday, I believe it is because I did not look hard enough or did not do enough to make the child known to the world.

My pushing led to an opportunity to have these three siblings videotaped and then to have their video, basically a commercial, aired on the news to help look for a family for them. We all really had great fun the day of the filming. The children, the adoption recruiting worker, a gentleman from the TV station, and I all went to the museum. The children played various activities and had a great time. When we were almost ready to leave, the newscaster sat down with the children and asked them what kind of family they would like to have. He clarified some of their responses so that the families watching would know what they wanted. What better way to know if you are going to be a good fit with a child than to know what the child wants and why he or she wants it. Both children provided many specifics things that would make up their perfect family: a home out of the state they were born in, a place with snow… Eddie stated that he wanted his own dog. The newscaster restated it by saying, "You want a family that allows pets." Eddie clarified and stated that it was OK for the family to have pets, but he wanted his own dog. He went on to explain that he has lived in many foster homes and most have had a dog, which he loved, fed, walked, and played with. The problem was that no matter how much he cared for the dog, it was still the foster parents' dog; when he changed homes, he lost his dog. Eddie stated that he wanted a dog that was all his. He wanted to be the sole owner and have all the responsibility for his dog. I do not believe the newscaster knew what to say about that. It was a statement that affected all of us adults. We just don't think about things like that. I may have thought, "It is just a dog," but when a child explains how important it is to have and be trusted with that type of responsibility, owning a pet takes on a whole new meaning.

I instructed the adoption recruiter to send me the home studies for the potential adoptive families as soon as possible so I could review them. The agency's policy is that an adoption staffing team meeting is held to review and consider all possible or prospective homes before a team decision is made. I believe that, especially given the age of my children, these kids should be a part of the decision process. This is not the case, though. Since I was going to be their only voice in the process, I needed to be prepared and ready to fight for what they wanted. I read through every home study and used a highlighter. I found that this was a great practice to stick with. In one color I highlight the positives, the qualities that align with the children's perfect family picture. I choose a different color to highlight concerns or questions that I need answered or addressed by the agency that completed the family's home study. I also attach another piece of paper with a summary of the good points, bad points, concerns, questions, and other notes that I thought would be handy in the staffing team meeting. Because I still believed that the final choice should be up to the children more than the adults, I wanted their input as well. I was not allowed to staff (that is, to discuss) each family with the children. I had to use the questions I ask the children (that I use regularly to this day) to figure out who they would choose if they were allowed to have a voice.

I reviewed seven home studies, with very different families in each one. I took the differences and compiled a list of questions for my children to narrow the choices. One family consisted of a mom and a dad; another was a same-sex couple. I then asked the children what kind of family they would choose. "If you could choose a family, would you want a mom and a dad, just a mom, just a dad, two dads, or two moms?"

The response was pretty amazing. They said, "A mom and a dad is OK as long as we do not ever have to be alone with the dad. If Mom goes to the store, we need to be able to go with her, and we do not want to come home from school with just Dad there. Just a mom would be OK, but two moms would be best; then there wouldn't be the worry about being alone with the dad."

Then I asked a follow-up question: whether they really knew what two moms meant a homosexual couple. The children's foster mother and their therapist asked again about their preference, to ensure that they understood before I went to battle. Many states, such as Texas, where we were located, do not allow same-sex adoptions or will allow only one of the parents to adopt. But before the adoption process began, I would have to get the approval to select the same-sex couple as the adoptive family and have a clear idea of which of the moms would be the legal, adoptive parent. This was not going to be an easy task. Because same-sex partners as adoptive parents are so controversial, I would not just have to build up all the positives of this one family but also break down every negative of the other six families. This was going to be downright hard.

I took on the challenge by taking out my highlighters and red pen. I highlighted all the key points of what made my same-sex couple the perfect match for these two children. Don't misinterpret me: I am not saying that only same-sex couples should adopt every child out of foster care. I am saying that there is a perfect family for every child, and for these particular siblings, this was and is the perfect family. Eddie doesn't just get his own dog that is his responsibility; he will get his own cat and horse too. They will have snow; they will be out of Texas and far from the abuse they have known for so long. They will not have a dad in the house but will have the opportunity to build healthy relationships with the many uncles, grandfathers, and male friends in the family so that one day they will feel safe in a home with men. The children have been identified as having special educational needs and will have a mom who is a teacher and specialized in special-needs children. How perfect is that? Despite all this perfection, the fight is still going to be big.

It is the day of the staffing. I am armed with my highlighted home studies and a novel of notes. The questions come at me from all directions. The first family that is reviewed I decline for the following reasons: Each parent has been married five times to other people. Each marriage has lasted no more than five to seven years before ending in divorce, and the spouses currently have been married to each other for only three years. I do not want my children living through years of abuse to then be in the middle of a divorce. The second family was just a dad—definitely a big NO; my children said so. End of discussion. Families two through six were in Texas (where there was no snow), had a large number of children in the home already, did not allow pets, were not willing to allow contact with the brother who would not be adopted with Abby and Eddie, and were not willing to keep in contact with the current foster parents whom the children are very attached to. Basically, these families provided a "no" to a large number of the items on the children's perfect family wish list. End of discussion.

Then we came to Jalyn and Rachel. They lived out of state where there was snow, they had pets, they would allow contact with the older brother and former foster parents, one was a teacher, there were no dads in the picture...the match seemed perfect, perfect, perfect.

Then other group members asked question after question. "Well, we see that Rachel has her master's degree. Don't you think that she will be too educated to be able to talk to a child with special educational needs?" *WHAT, are you serious?* I thought but never said out loud. My verbal response was: "Her master's degree is in *education*, and she teaches at a Montessori school where the children would get much more specialized care and education." *Next comment?* "I don't know if their relationship is very stable." (I know that concern came up because I tore apart the frequent divorces of the first couple.) My response: "Jalyn and Rachel have been in a committed relationship for thirteen years. Their stability and commitment to each other, though not easy in a society that is not always accepting of homosexuality, is a statement to their character and commitment to the children they will adopt, as society also does not always accept adoption or all the baggage that our children carry." I thought to myself, good answer, *Next?* "Do you really think that the children will want to be raised by two women? How hard will that be: to have to explain to your friends that your mothers are gay?" My answer: "I have already asked the children, and they both, independently of each other, stated that they would prefer to have two moms as opposed to a house with a dad that they may have to be alone with. I concluded that the bottom line in this debate is that the children's voice shall be heard and their wishes known and respected."

At the end of the day, when all was said and done, I made the best phone call ever. I informed Jalyn and Rachel that they were going to be mommies. I would have sworn they were going to jump right through the phone, they were so excited. I explained to them the next step of the process: informing the children and setting up some time for them to get to know each other better. This would start with phone calls. Once they could make arrangements to come to Texas, we would schedule some time for them to be together.

There are some foster parents who are very helpful in transitioning children to their adoptive homes. Ms. Violet was just that foster parent. I called her as soon as a decision was made. I explained to her that a family had been selected for Abby and Eddie. I explained that their request to never have to come home to a father, and to be able to go shopping with the mother so they were not home alone with a father at any time, had resulted in the selection of two moms. I further explained that they were a same-sex couple. I asked Ms. Violet if she thought, in the long time that the children had been in her home, they truly understood what having two moms meant—two moms in this case would mean the moms are gay. She stated that she believed they understood this, but she would start talking with them about this to help them understand. (Ms. Violet called later in the week and shared with me that the kids watched a TV show with her that showed a gay couple adopting a baby. She stated that after the show, the kids said they thought that was very cool.) She shared that they talked for quite a while about what it would be like to have moms who were gay. They talked about how other kids might look at them for having two moms. They talked about how they would feel, comments that other kids might make, how they would respond, and, most importantly, if this was something they thought they could handle or would even want. Ms. Violet shared that both children appeared to have a very clear understanding of what this would mean and both were very open to the idea. She stated that they both indicated that this is really what they wanted because it would mean they would never have a father to come home to or be left alone with. Ms. Violet informed them that just the lack of a dad didn't mean that there wouldn't be grandpas or uncles or male friends in the picture. The children shared that at least they would have a say as to whether or not they had to be alone with these men.

The following week I went out to see the children. I took with me several photos that Jalyn and Rachel had provided of themselves, their family, their horses, and, of course, the dogs. The children were so excited to start talking to their mom and mommy, as they had determined they would distinguish between the two mothers. I provided the foster mother the phone number and contact information for the adoptive family. Phone calls and letters could start immediately, and they did. I do believe that they talked almost daily. Jalyn and Rachel could hardly wait to meet their children face-to-face. They scheduled a visit during spring break, when Jalyn and the children would be out of school, so they could all spend plenty of time together. The visit went great but made it very difficult for them to return home and leave their children in Texas. The strong bond and desire to be together as a family meant that the next step could not be slowed down for any reason. When it comes to permanency for my children, I can sometimes get a little pushy, and I did get pushy in this case. Jalyn and Rachel were not new at pushing people around either. They made some phone calls; I pushed and pushed on the adoption worker to get placement in the adoptive home as soon as possible.

It was determined that a good time to transition the children was as soon as school was out for the summer. I was not happy to find out that the placement is done by the adoption worker, not by the assigned worker, me, who had fought so hard to put this family together. Policy is policy, though; I had to step aside. Luckily, it just happened that the adoption worker broke her foot the week before the placement. A substitute would have to travel out of state with the children to do the placement. Guess who volunteered? You guessed it: me. This was the children's first airplane ride; the journey was pure excitement put on top of the overwhelming excitement of going home for good, to their last placement ever. *Wow.*

When we finally arrived at their new home, everything was in place and ready for the children's arrival, all with the exception of Eddie's bed. They had already discussed this with the children prior to their arrival; Rachel and Eddie were going to build his very own loft bed from wood beams. The children were introduced to their new pets and chose which ones belonged to whom. It was more like the dogs and cats chose which child belonged to them. There were instant attractions all over the place. It was very clear that some adjustments would need to be made, but these children were in fact home. One adjustment for the new mom and mommy was having meat in the house, and of all things, hot dogs.

⇥ ⇤

We are Jalyn and Rachel, or Mom and Mommy, as we prefer to be called now. It is an amazing feeling being a family all of a sudden. We have considered adopting for so long. We have looked at hundreds of children on various websites in just about every state. We have inquired about so many children and have been rejected numerous times for a multitude of reasons, some of which we were never even explained. We firmly believe that there were at least two great reasons why all the other children did not work out for us and why our family took so long to happen: we just hadn't found the right children, and they hadn't found us. Not everyone is open to a lesbian couple adopting, and we are sure there are many children who would not be OK with it. Our children needed two moms as much as we needed them. Oh, believe us when we say it was not just by chance that we found each other. It was by a lot of caring and hard work by a caseworker who listened to her children. We are sure that there are many other children who may have hoped and prayed to find us, but they did not have someone to listen to what they really wanted. Our children were very lucky.

We have had Abby and Eddie for six years now. Their caseworker from all those years ago asked us to allow them to be included in this book. What better way is there to say thank you to the person who brought us together to be a family than to tell our story? What better way to help other children and their parents who are still looking for each other than to share our amazing journey? Their caseworker is correct, and right on the money, in believing that forever families change the lives of children. We are in awe daily about the changes that we have had the privilege of watching over the past six years.

Our children came to us with a case file to review that was nine inches thick for each child. That is nine inches worth of history in foster care; nine inches of documentation of abuse and neglect; nine inches of documentation of diagnosis; nine inches of educational delays and special educational plans; nine inches of baggage that we could not imagine carrying as adults, let alone as children. Neither of us is sure that we could have survived the history that our children have lived through. We have read about and know the trauma that they have endured. We could see why there was a need for therapy, medication, and special education. We also had to see if there was something better for our children than more doctors, more therapists, more special-education classes, more, more, more. Maybe all they needed was two: two parents who love them unconditionally, two parents who would stick with them no matter what, two parents who would help with their homework, two parents they could talk to and who would listen, two parents who would not give up on them. Maybe all they needed was the two of us.

OK, please don't start writing the publisher and complaining that these women are crazy because they took away medication and therapy and special education from children who had been diagnosed for years and needed this professional help. We did no such thing. We did, however, listen to our children and followed where they led. We worked with them in reading, math, science, and so on, and when they were back on track and had met all of the educational expectations of their grade level, we moved with them past the need for special-education classes. We did, however, listen to our children and watched as they changed. We requested that the doctor try lower doses of medication so that they were receiving only what they needed to be stable and calm. We listened when our children stated that they didn't really think they needed the medication anymore, and we talked to their doctors, who tried not giving them medication. We celebrated with our children when we all realized that there was no longer a need or place in their lives for medication to make them feel better; to make them not always feel sad, oppositional, defiant, hyper, and unable to pay attention. We listened to our children when they stated that they preferred to talk to us when they had a problem or concern or when they needed to sort through stuff. We celebrated with our children when we all realized that their mom and mommy could fill the shoes of a therapist and listen and provide feedback. We took nothing away from our children that they had not already lost a need for. You would not force your children to continue to wear braces on their teeth after they are already straight and perfect; they now have retainers to keep their teeth that way. Our children had worn their braces: therapist, medication, Individual Education Plan (IEP). Their retainer now is the love and support they get every day in our family.

We received Abby and Eddie with ADHD, bipolar disorder, oppositional defiant disorder, mild mental retardation, PTSD, and a Global Assessment of Functioning (GAF) of forty. Today we have two children who are on the A honor roll and are clear of diagnoses and medications. We do, however, have teenagers with teenage problems: problems with choosing positive friends to hang out with, but they have overcome that; problems with arguing over how much time they can spend on the phone, but they listen anyway; problems planning their time so that they are not up way past bedtime finishing a school project, but they finish it; problems getting in on time for curfew, but they make it with a minute to spare. We have teenagers who had a very heavy load to carry. It was too much to carry by themselves, and it weighed them down so much that they could barely move forward. We helped carry their baggage. Unfortunately, we could not throw all things in the load away, though we would love to. Fortunately, carrying it together has lightened the load to the point that it can be put aside for today but we can still learn from all that it holds.

Adopting our children, Abby and Eddie, changed our lives in so many ways. We cannot up and take a weekend away from them or be reckless in any way. We have to be true adults all the time. But our children have made us better people. We have seen their changes, but we are the ones who received the greatest gift by their loving and choosing us, not the other way around. We wish that every family that is looking for a child to adopt would not look for the child or children that fit their perfect picture. Instead, you must look for the child that makes your pictures perfect. Those children will know you when they find you. It is we adoptive parents that need to stay open.

Many years have passed since our children came into our lives and our hearts. We have stood by each other through many happy times: good grades, having a homecoming-queen ego in our midst, graduations...We have had many struggles with choosing negative friends and partners in life. We all entered this family for both good and bad, and we have held each other up through it all. There was a period of time during which our daughter thought that moms were no longer something she needed. But we learned from a talk with our caseworker from so many years ago that she too has shared the same struggle with her own daughter—and she gave birth to her.

Today, we celebrate a new family member. We are no longer just moms to two amazing kids who had a rough start; we are now grandparents to the most precious little man. It is our hope and our prayers now and forever that the cycle of violence that our children entered this world with has been wiped clear, not just broken but shattered. Our daughter's beautiful baby boy will never know the abuse and neglect that his mother endured. She is new at this mommy thing, but she has already demonstrated that no one or anything will be allowed to hurt him. Her love for him surpasses all else.

Update: Since the original completion of the manuscript, immediately prior to the publication. Both siblings have children on their own that are now four years old. Their children have not experienced any of the abuse or neglect that their parents and even grandparents knew. The love that Abby and Eddie received from their adoptive parents and extended family has taught them what true, unconditional love is. They live each day loving their own children with unconditional love, putting their children first and making sure that they are free from abuse and neglect.

CHAPTER 3
RYAN AND BRIAN

Hi, **I am Ryan**. I have two sisters. I can't say that I remember everything about when I first came into foster care. I have been told that I was only three years old the first time that a social worker took me from my parents. I have been told that it was just my father then; my mother had already left me behind. It has been many years ago, and I have no clue what the actual reason was. While I have been in and out of foster care for a while, I can tell you I haven't really understood everything that has happened. I can tell you I have lived with the man I thought was my father, even though I have since been told he may really not be; but the court has said that he is, and I guess that is all that matters. I have lived with my so-called aunt, but if my father is not really my father, then she probably isn't my aunt either. I actually got to be with my sisters when we were living with the aunt. I know that I was pretty screwed up then and threatened to kill her. Obviously, this didn't go over real well, so I got kicked out and went to a foster home. I have no clue how many of those I have had 'cause they are pretty much the same. They pretend that they care; they feed me, send me to school, and are supposed to provide me clothes. Just like my aunt, they bail out when I screw up. I get in fights at school—get sent to juvenile detention for fighting, stealing, threatening people, and a bunch of stuff. I really get pushed off to a new foster home if I test limits. You see, when no one has ever loved you, you start to act really bad to see if this one might be different. They never are. All of 'em have proved that they are the same.

I have figured out that I am not the same as all the other kids that have been in my foster homes. I keep asking for a social security card and state ID. There have been lots of social workers in my life, and they have all been pretty lame, in my opinion. They say that my social security card, state ID, and even my birth certificate are being worked on, but how is it that everyone else has them? School keeps asking for mine, and it is never around. 'K, it was finally figured out that 'cause I wasn't born in the United States, I don't get one. How is that? The man the court says is my father is American, so I should be. They must all think that I am stupid or something. The fact is that I am smarter than them—all the foster parents, teachers, and especially those social workers. So 'cause of their stupidity, I can't have all the papers and stuff that make you somebody in this world. Whatever. If I can be adopted, then I can get my social security card, a new birth certificate without the name of the man who isn't really my father, and maybe even a driver's license instead of just a state ID.

This is how this went. The court got rid of the man they decided was my father. I made it real clear that I wanted a real family, not these foster families that don't give a damn. One social worker is in charge of that, so *again* I got a new social worker. Told you they were pretty stupid if they can only do one thing. Shouldn't they be trained to do whatever us kids need? Whatever. Well, this one must be smarter than the rest. The social worker actually found me a family who says they are actually going to stick around. It must be true 'cause I got sent to a new state for this family. Maybe that has been the problem all along. This state is the stupid one and needs other states to get things done. So off I go. I am so excited to think that I may actually be out of the system after all these years of bouncing around from home to home. I will even get a social security card and at this point that means a *car*—woohoo!

I told you once before that I really don't trust people and I believe they all need to be tested. If this family can't be scared off, maybe it will be forever. So I did think for a little while maybe this is perfect and I should just behave and skip the test. She, the mother (no dad in this home), is very smart and has done more than just feed me. She has shown me how much she loves me. I can't help myself. She must be tested. How else am I going to know that she loves me? So here is how it went. I pushed and acted a little crazy. She got me help: meds, inpatient counseling. So far she is passing the test, but if I was going to keep her and make her my mom, then she really had to pass with flying colors. I pulled out all the stops and threatened her with a knife. Maybe that was a little extreme, but as I have been shown before, she ran for the hills. Dammit, I was right. Back to foster care I go.

Guess what. I was right on all counts. I get more stupid social workers. I get a new one yet again. I overheard them say that I am "unadoptable." What the hell does that mean? Does that mean that they are all useless and can't do their jobs? I am smarter than all the adults that I have had in my life, so it must be their lack of abilities, not that I can't be loved by anyone. That is crazy to even think about. I have seen other kids in foster care be loved by people. My sisters, who I now haven't seen or even heard from for years, have our aunt, and she loves them. We are siblings, so obviously we have some the same stuff inside. If they are lovable, then so am I. How could they say that I am "unadoptable"? They obviously didn't know I was listening or just don't care that I know what they say about me. You know what this means? More testing will have to take place to make sure that the next family proves they know I am worthy of love.

⊷ ⊶

OK, so I am Brian. I don't really know the reason I came into foster care. I know my twin brother and our older brother all got taken from our mother when I was very little. We have an aunt in a really warm place, and she was willing to take care of us. I have been told that our mom was hurting us because of her drug use and people she hangs out with—whatever that means. Anyway, we all went to our aunt. I think I was maybe five, maybe not. I can't even tell you how long I lived with my aunt and uncle or what really went wrong. She was really mean and thought that hitting us was OK when we were bad. How is it that they say my mom was "hurting" us, but I don't remember her ever hitting us? How it is that getting hit again and again by our aunt is OK? All of these people in charge must know best, but this doesn't feel better. I hurt all the time and cry myself to sleep.

One day these new people came to my aunt's house. They were like the ones in the cold and wet place we lived before. This time they only took me away. I want them to take my twin with me. It is not right that he gets to stay with my aunt and I don't. I guess that is because I was the only one who got hit. I must have done something wrong and must have deserved to be hit. Now that I know what is expected of me, the rest of this should be easy to get through; whatever "this" is. I don't know what I was doing wrong, so I will have to try different things that are bad so maybe I can go back and see my twin.

I started with one social worker and a foster home. This is not my aunt or anyone I know. They seem nice, but like I told you, I already know that I am expected to be bad. The question is "Where to start?" I have to go to school every day, so I will try some tricks there. I pushed some other kids in line. It is stupid to have to stand in a line to go pee. There is no line at the foster home. If you have to pee, you go. I have to go so I just pushed the rest of the kids out of my way. The foster parents got called and had to leave work to come get me. They looked pretty mad at me. Ta-da, I figured this out really quick. I got them mad just like my aunt. I know I am going to get hit and then I will go back to see my twin. *Wrong!* They yell a lot but no hitting. OK, I will try something else. I get to go to school again, so I hit a kid. He looked at me weird and deserved it. Besides, I have to go see my brother; I miss him. Again the school calls the foster parents, who are really mad now 'cause they had to leave work again. Having them really mad means I should really really get hit this time. I know I will get to see my brother now. But *nope!* My social worker lady does show up at the foster home, though, and I get in her car. She must be taking me to my brother. *Double nope!* Even though it is really late at night, I am taken to a new foster home, and the next day a new school. Whatever. They have kids I can hit also. You guessed it: I started there. This time I hit a girl. I am taken to the office. It looks the same but has different people than the last school. This time they make me go to a special room. I wait for the foster parents to come and pick me up. They will have to leave work, will get pissed off, and I will go to see my brother. Being sent to this special room must have been the step I missed at the last school. But all I get is sent home after school. The foster parents don't say anything about it. I am totally confused. The next day at school, I start in the special room with other kids. You guessed it. I hit one of them. You will not believe it, but this kid hits me back. Oh, it is on. I get a few hits in before we are separated by the teacher. *Ha ha*, I get to go back to the office. Now I will see my brother. This time the social worker shows up, and there are a bunch of people talking in the other room. They must be talking about how to send me to my brother. I am so confused. I just get sent to a special class. This isn't working. The whole school thing isn't getting me to my brother, and I can't wait.

New day, different plan. I am told to go to school. *No way.* School isn't the place to get me sent to my brother. Today I stay in bed and refuse to go. The foster parents figure I am just sick, so they don't go to work and stay home with me. They seem to really care. Maybe they will just bring my brother to me. I never thought about that. This will work. I refuse to go to school for the next few days. They take me to the doctor. He says that there is nothing wrong with me, so I get dragged to school. *Fine.* I take a kitchen knife to school and try to threaten the teachers and students. I really don't want to hurt them for real, but they need to know I am serious. Today the social worker and foster parents come to school. I leave with the social worker, not the foster parents. I have to sit at her office for a while, and then she takes me to a new foster home. What the hell is this? My plan is never going to work if I have to start at the beginning every time I get moved.

This new foster home is really strict and makes me go and talk to some strange man a couple times a week. I am so confused. I try to explain to this man who calls himself my therapist what my plan is. He says that is not how it works. I try and explain that I need to see my brother. He tries to explain that this will never happen. Now I have to take pills that will make me behave. *Really?* I don't understand any of this anymore. I tell him, the foster parents, and social worker they can't stop me from seeing my brother. My plan *will work.* I am tougher than they are.

It has now been twenty foster homes and schools later. I am still trying. It has now been eight or nine years since I have seen my brother. I can't even remember what he looks like. I have had at least seven social workers that I can remember. They say that I can be adopted if I want. I go to a new foster home where they say that they will love me forever and want to adopt me. I have heard this before. It is never true. It never gets me to my brother. It is always taken back the minute I go to juvy again or get kicked out of school. I even went to a meeting at the social worker's office where I heard them talking. I hear everything, regardless of what they think. I heard them say that I am "unadoptable." They talk about me staying with the current family forever but with some type of court papers, not adoption. I don't get it but know that this won't work either.

I have figured it out. Seeing my brother is going to have to wait until we are adults. Maybe if someone had told me that when I was little, I wouldn't have had so many foster homes, schools, and social workers.

Is it possible to tell people that the state is technically your parents? That is just wrong, but the therapist said that my mom and the guy who was my father are no longer my parents. Someone has to be, 'cause all kids have parents, so mine must be social workers and the judge or maybe my probation officer. The foster parents don't claim me, so it can't be them. I don't seem to know anything these days, and I don't remember a whole lot of my real family, so I can tell people what I want.

"I'ma gangsta. I sell *drugs*. I use *drugs*. I screw all the beautiful girls and they *worship* me."

"My family is with the mob; don't even mess with me."

I have told the stories so many times; it must be true, right? Maybe if all my stories were just that, someone would really love me and I could stop with all the foster homes, schools, social workers, saying good-bye to every friend, and actually see my brother.

I got yet another social worker today. She seems different. She talks to me and seems to listen. Well, she can actually repeat what I say and asks questions that go with what I have said. Maybe she is different. Maybe she will find me a real family. *Maybe.*

She has been asking all sorts of questions. She wants to know where I want to live, and what parents look like—but not hair color, eye color, or how tall they are. She asked a weird question: "Is a family a mom and a dad? Is a family just a mom? Is a family just a dad?" How the hell am I supposed to know? I haven't had a family since I was five.

It has been a few weeks since I met her, and she made her usual monthly visit. Today she asked if I thought two dads equals a family? I was confused at first and then asked if that meant they were gay. She said, "Yes."

I thought long and hard and then said, "Well, if they were my family, then it would be better." She asked, "Why would it make things better?"

I explained, "People have made fun and picked on me forever because I am a foster kid. People always pick on and make fun of people that are gay." I explained, "We are both different, and people don't like different. Maybe there would be safety in numbers."

She told me that was a very grown-up way to look at things. No one has ever told me that I act like a grown-up. To be honest, I have never given anyone reason to think I can act grown-up.

⇒╪ ╪⇐

I am the social worker. I have just been assigned two cases. Regardless of what I have read in the entire two file drawers, they are not brothers. They do not share the same biological mothers or even fathers. They were not born even in the same country, let alone the same state. Though inspirational message of this book may lead you to hope otherwise, they were not adopted into the same family either. They have not even shared the same foster home at any time. So you ask, how it is that an educated social worker would believe that they could be brothers if they don't have the same birth or adoptive parents, birthdays or birthplaces, or foster homes, and if they don't even consider each other best friends? How are they brothers?

Ryan and Brian came into care three days apart. They have each had more social workers than they can count. To say they have had a lot of social workers is an understatement, but these social workers make up a very short list compared to the number of foster homes Ryan and Brian have been placed in. They have been raised by the same parents: Children's Administration and a long list of their social workers. They have so much in common that anyone with half a brain would say, "Those two are brothers." Special education has been a part of their lives for as long as they can remember. There are a lot of kids who have to be in special education because of their IQs, but not them. They are very bright and intelligent young men. If they behaved long enough, they might even be smart enough for one of those honors classes.

Ryan actually knows that he is smarter than anyone in the school, including most, if not all, of the teachers. I can already hear your question: "So why special education? Well, you see, the public school system has issues with kids who act out. It is not like either one of them liked getting into trouble. (OK, maybe there was a part of them that did like getting into trouble.) When a child is in trouble all the time at school, he or she is put in one of these "self-contained" classrooms. They are full of kids just like that first child, and maybe there is safety in numbers. If everyone in the class has behavior problems, then they all get to blend in with the troublemaker group and don't have to worry about people wanting to be their friends. You see, making friends seems like a waste of time and energy for these kids. If they have real friends, then those friends will want to know more about them: their family, where they grew up, their siblings…Explaining about their foster parents has only caused people to make fun of them or pity them. Besides, they will be changing schools soon enough anyway, so once again, why should they bother?

Ryan and Brian's uncanny resemblance is also striking in that they've both been through all this; they both even hang out at juvenile detention frequently. But there is this little issue with hanging out in the special-education classes. Even Ryan and Brian can only handle so much bad behavior. Safety in numbers isn't always so safe. Come to find out, even the other kids with behavior problems like to make fun of foster kids with social workers for "parents." There must be some safety in numbers at juvenile detention since the court sees so many foster kids; the officials there have already assigned the exact same probation officer just for foster kids The judges really do care and seem to feel sorry for those poor kids with no parents, but the courts can't really hold parents accountable for these kinds of kids' actions like they do for all the other kids around here. So as long as the last foster home is willing to take foster kids back or the social worker has a new home for them, the court is willing to cut a foster kid loose. Nine times out of ten, a stopover at juvenile detention will surely mean a new foster home. Foster children seem happy they didn't make any friends at the last school. Being on the move again, they wouldn't have been allowed to say good-bye or explain why they were leaving.

Violence has become second nature to kids like Ryan and Brian. When kids at school make fun of the fact that someone is a foster kid, they are just asking for trouble. When those other kids at the new foster home think that since another kid is the newbie, his or her stuff is free for the taking, they are just asking for trouble.

I have my work cut out for me. I have never believed the statement that a child is "unadoptable." I can see the small child in every teenager who has long passed the "perfect age" for adoption. I can see these kids' desire to be loved. I hear it in their stories and answers to every question. They want nothing in this world more than to be loved forever. They each have their own wish list for a family. Every item is unique to just them. You see, they may share experiences, but Ryan and Brian are not brothers. They are individuals who want to have their very own family.

Brian sees safety in numbers and wouldn't mind gay dads. Ryan wants nothing to do with homosexuality. Ryan needs someone as smart as or smarter than he is, though he will tell you that person doesn't exist. Brian's reply to whether he wants a family whose parents are educated is "Whatever." Ryan's list of characteristics of a perfect family is so long that it is a little overwhelming. Brian's is short and to the point; he wants someone to love him.

Each child has his own set of baggage and obstacles to get around or through in order get him home. For Ryan, a social security card, which is unattainable until we can prove citizenship, ends up being an obstacle that is overwhelming, frustrating, and almost impossible. With the help of a coworker who was originally from Canada, we were able to obtain an original birth certificate. This was only one of many steps, but one that had been impossible to complete for the many social workers who had been a part of this child's life for over eight years.

The next step seemed easy enough, at least on paper. The correct form for special immigration juvenile status (SIJS) had to be completed. It had to be easy enough. Since there isn't a special worker assigned to such cases, anyone should be able to do it. I received the monthly e-mails notifying me that Ryan didn't have a social security number (SSN) in the computer, and every month I would respond with "Requires SIJS." I was sure that if there was this urgent need for the SSN to be in the computer and there was, in fact, a specialist to handle these cases, then I would have been informed. Since there was no notification even when I requested additional assistance, there must not be anyone. Once again, I interpreted this to mean that it couldn't be that hard. I located the SIJS forms, which are specifically for children in foster care who have experienced abuse/neglect and who now have the state as their legal guardian. With the utmost care, I completed the form, attached the legal documents and birth certificate, and mailed it as registered return receipt; I was not taking any chances. Within less than a month, I received a special envelope from the Department of Immigration. Knowing that this was an easy process, I was immediately jumping up and down knowing that I had been successful. I was wrong, though! Immigration was requesting additional information. First, documentation from the court had to state that Ryan was a ward of the state. Done. The second required document had to state that he could not return to his biological parents. Done: we had terminated parental rights; of course he couldn't return. Document number three had to say that he would not be able to obtain permanency without citizenship. I really thought that this was all self-explanatory with the original legal documents I had sent, but I would do whatever it took. I requested a special court hearing and requested one court order that spelled out exactly what Immigration had requested. Once this court order was obtained, I resubmitted it with all the other documentation and special forms.

Another couple of weeks went by, and I received another special envelope from Immigration. I was equally excited as I knew that I had finally sent exactly what Immigration wanted. Wrong answer yet again! Now there was a new request for additional documentation regarding the biological parents. Someone needs to explain a few things to me: (1) why can't Immigration make all of its requests at one time and save the state and federal government some postage, and (2) why doesn't the state have someone special to handle SIJS? This is obviously not as simple as sending in a form. I made one more try with additional documentation to include the biological mother's and father's birth certificates. But this produced the same results: a special envelope and additional requests.

At this point I started seriously looking for reinforcements. I was told by a coworker that one of the attorneys who represent the children in foster care had experience with immigration matters. The attorney then stated that he was not my man but instead suggested a nonprofit organization, whose name he couldn't remember, in Seattle that helped with SIJS. *Google, here I come!* Searching for "SIJS + Seattle brought me to Northwest Immigrant Rights Project at www.immigrationadvocates.org. Now maybe we could get somewhere. This organization was the specialist that I needed all along. I started where all good research starts, with an e-mail. E-mail correspondence allows me to have a paper trail. This way, when my monthly reminder that Ryan didn't have an SSN came across my desk, I could prove that I was trying. I received an almost immediate response. Mike, the specialist, and I were in what seemed like constant communication. E-mail and phone calls took place several times a week. I scanned and e-mailed him all the documentation that I had gathered. He was amazed at all the leg work I had already done. He apologized when he had to inform me that even with all that I had in hand, it still wasn't going to be a quick process.

A father for Ryan was identified. Once Ryan's possible new dad gave Ryan permission to read his home study, Ryan approved. Ryan is a very smart young man and figures if someone who is going to be his dad is allowed to read every detail of his life, then Ryan should be allowed to read everything about the man he may call "Dad." True love is seeing the heavy baggage, knowing that this is going to be a long process because of citizenship and social security cards. He takes on the test of loving Ryan anyway. Ryan was placed in his prospective adoptive father's home on his sixteenth birthday. What a present!

Mike and I continued to work at obtaining Ryan's naturalization. It is sad to say, but Ryan's biological mother had been the US citizen rather than his father, his naturalization would have been automatic. Since his biological father had been the American citizen, though, there was more documentation than I could have even imagined. We had to prove that the father had lived in the United States for five consecutive years prior to Ryan's birth. We had legal documents: jail records and proof of social security checks that he had received for mental health disability. However, these didn't prove that he was actually residing in the United States for five consecutive years. Immigration's logic was that the social security checks could have been received by someone else while he resided out of country. The jail time was only a snapshot of the amount of time he was in jail total, and it didn't equal five consecutive years. *Think, think, think,* I demanded of myself. What would that kind of proof look like: church attendance, rental agreements, or employment? His housing situation was choppy, and the identified church refused to provide any assistance due to confidentiality. Because the state had terminated his parental rights, the father refused to be helpful. Mike determined he could actually request information from the biological father by stating he was just trying to help Ryan become a citizen, which had nothing to do with the state—all of which was true. Mike just left out that in becoming a citizen, Ryan could also be adopted. It was worth a shot, and it was the only shot we had.

Miracle of all miracles, the biological father agreed to release his employment records to the Special Immigration Project. Finally, the complete packet was sent. I notified Ryan and his prospective father of the progress. Now we were all crossing our fingers, saying prayers, lighting candles, and anything else that could be thought of.

After all the e-mails, phone conversations, hunting of documentation, prayers, and crossed fingers, an e-mail arrived one morning. I couldn't help but sit with the biggest smile on my face and tears running down my cheeks. Even today as I am in the middle of writing this book, the tears have started again and the chills run up and down my body. I had received an invitation to Ryan's citizenship swearing-in ceremony. I couldn't believe it. I started dialing every number I had for Ryan's prospective adoptive father: work, home, cell. I finally left a message that simply said, "Please call me as soon as possible. It is very important." Within five minutes I received a call back. I couldn't hold the tears back for even a second while I got the words out of my mouth. I simply asked if he was in front of a computer as I was sending him an e-mail that he needed to read while on the phone with me. He received it within minutes, and we shared the tears.

The day had come. Ryan stood before a crowd of people—family, friends, and me. He took his oath and posed for photos. We had made it through the biggest obstacle, citizenship. Now we only had to obtain an SSN and set a court date for adoption. We didn't waste any time. We left the Immigration Department and went immediately to the Social Security Administration. With the ink still wet on Ryan's naturalization certificate, and with Ryan's birth certificate and court documents, plus my state identification badge in hand, we requested Ryan's very own SSN. Four weeks passed before the mail arrived at the office. You guessed it—there were more tears, more phone calls. This time all that was needed was a date for adoption. Ryan picked his day and decided that since he had entered the world of his biological parents on his birthday, the best way to start anew and clear the past was to be adopted on his seventeenth birthday. Babies are not the only ones who are adopted.

In contrast, Brian's obstacles seemed a little less overwhelming, since he already had an SSN and was born a citizen. Working in a state that is very open-minded about same-sex couples adopting made it even easier. When a family is found in a state that has laws against same-sex couples adopting, life becomes hell, and finalizing the family's unity seems an impossible goal to achieve. I am a firm believer that, as corny as it may sound, love for a child can move mountains, and the love of a parent can empty baggage and heal wounds.

⇥ ⇤

Enter stage right: another character to this tragic, comic love story. **I am James.** I have been pulled into the life of Ryan. As is policy with the Department of Child Services, I have been provided lengthy documentation about a child whom I was considering for adoption. I must admit, it was very overwhelming. I couldn't go there. This was too much baggage, too much to take on. I was not up for that kind of challenge. I quickly notified the social worker that I was not, could not, be the father for this poor child. I have worked in the department before and know that it's standard for documentation to be returned when a family is no longer under consideration, but I was so overwhelmed by what I had read, it didn't even cross my mind to send it back. It got thrown in a pile of other papers next to my bed. (I am such an organized person.)

I have this really big problem of grabbing things to read in the middle of the night when I can't sleep. Since Ryan's documentation was on top of a stack of very "organized" reading materials, it ended up in my line of sight. I started reading again. "Really, why would I even bother?" I was overwhelmed the first time I read it. What would make a second read any different? I have been a social worker for most of my adult life; I understand these situations. But as I read through the pages and pages of words that convinced me previously that I couldn't do this, I realized something. How many times have I read someone else's truths? How many times have I actually gotten to know people and realized that not everything is as it seems? How many times have I given people who appeared awful a chance to prove the world wrong? Why is this child any different? Shouldn't I at least meet him? He isn't a case file. He isn't words on a page. He is a kid who has been looking for someone to love him. I should be willing to at least say, "Hi."

I sent out an e-mail to the social worker whom I had previously told not only "no" but "hell no." The idea of notifying her of my change of heart was too much to take, so I didn't even wait for morning. I typed a 2:00 a.m. e-mail and sent it immediately. I thought, *She really will question her choice in even considering a crazy man who sends e-mails this early and who can't even make up his mind.* Her response later in the day took me by surprise. She thanked me for my reconsideration and stated that she was glad that she hadn't requested Ryan's file back. She stated that it was her hope that I would take a second look. Then I thought, *OK, so she is even crazier than those of us who send 2:00 a.m. e-mails!*

Within a few days, I was asked if Ryan could read my home study, to which I said, "Of course." I got to read about him and make my own first impressions; he should get the same courtesy. A few more days passed. Then, out of the blue, I received a call from the social worker. *Man, this social worker works fast,* I thought. I was anticipating the month-long wait, holding my breath, questioning my decision to even meet Ryan, planning what I would say, and planning what we would do. How could I soak all this in and take a breath when it had only been two days since I informed the social worker I was willing to, at bare minimum, meet Ryan? The social worker stated that Ryan had read the home study and was interested in meeting me. Ryan asked that the social worker to warn me that this was the biggest test I would ever have to pass and I should be ready. The social worker suggested that we do an activity that would be more than just a meal. She explained that sitting across a table with no activity other than eating can prove to be very awkward, like a first date. Instead, she had a fun date planned—bowling. Knowing that Ryan believes that all adults are lacking in IQ, I came prepared with a brain teaser. I had read that if you weave two phone books together, they cannot be separated, so I brought two phone books so that, if Ryan wanted, we could put this theory to the test. We paid for the bowling and then got our shoes and our lane. When we sat down I shared the test with Ryan and stated that if he was interested, we could try it after we were finished bowling. He decided that the experiment was much more interesting than bowling, so we sat at the funky little bowling table talking and weaving the phone books. *Wow*, how could I be so wrong? This kid is amazing. It was almost like we were always family, but the universe made a mistake by taking so long to get us together. From our first meeting, things seemed to move like a whirlwind.

In no time Ryan joined my household, and we started to get to really know each other. As expected, the tests started almost immediately. Some intentional damage to my car was first. "Sorry, Ryan," I responded, "but it is just a car and replaceable." Then came destruction of a more prized possession, my collection of planes. Once again, though it was more upsetting, his attempt to push me away did not work.

Most placements in a prospective adoptive home go pretty fast, but as you have previously read, Ryan had a small problem with citizenship that seemed to drag on forever. There must have been some powers at work or maybe just a stubborn social worker. But I figured out that our social worker was unrelenting when it came to kids on her workload. As I previously shared, I have worked for the department before and am all too aware of things not working out as planned. I was prepared for the fact that Ryan would never have citizenship prior to turning eighteen, that the adoption wouldn't be able to be finalized, and that we would have to figure things out on our own once the state left his life when he was eighteen. Soon, though, I realized that "unrelenting" is an understatement when describing our social worker. From her, every social worker could learn a few things about caring for the children on his or her workload; every child deserves a family, a positive future, and a life without the state and the courts as his or her parents. Ryan and I were blessed to share his citizenship ceremony, applying for his social security card, and, miracle of all miracles, adoption finalization on Ryan's seventeenth birthday.

It has been over two years since he came to me, and I cannot imagine a life without him. To all the people who have come and gone throughout his life, we have some news for you: Ryan was "adoptable," but if you had stayed in his life, I never would have fallen in love with such an amazing young man. Shame on all of you for holding Ryan back from being the amazing young man that he is today. You need to know that he is in regular, not self-contained, classes; he is on the A honor roll; he has healthy peer relationships; he is the safest teen driver I have ever known; and he has not seen a juvenile detention center or psych inpatient unit since he arrived in my life. Shame on all of you for stealing him away from a loving family for so many years. I do have to thank you, though. If you hadn't kept a hold on him for so long, we never would have found the amazing love that a father and son can have.

As an update to the reader, Ryan has now graduated from high school just prior to the publication of this book. He did have an unexpected turn—a situation that he had to confront. A few days before his graduation, his birth father tracked him down somehow. He called and requested to talk to and see Ryan. Ryan is a much stronger young man than anyone would have ever imagined he could be. As his dad, I can tell you that this was a very difficult situation. Ryan had a minor meltdown and initially was very upset, scared, and confused as to what to do. But, as I just stated, he is an amazingly strong young man. He knew he could talk to me. Though I sought some advice from his old social worker (who never cuts ties with her kids and is always available for questions and support, and loves the updates), it was not needed in the long run. Ryan came to the same conclusion that the social worker had provided in her advice. He came to me, we talked it through, and he chose to leave his past right where it was—in the past. He explained to the "father," "You have no place in my life, and you can just #$%* off."

Ryan knows the importance of having a voice and believes that people need to hear what he has to say. As a US citizen, he is determined to talk to his congressman and senators. He is an activist for change. Ryan will be starting school again in the fall. I know that *my son* will be changing the world and is able to do this because he was provided a chance to be loved and have a family.

Not all families choose to keep in their lives the social worker who facilitated the making of their family possible. For many it is a constant reminder of the negative life that was left behind. However, others enjoy keeping in touch and providing updates as a symbol of gratitude for the work that brought them together. Ryan's adoptive father sends periodic updates about his son's major accomplishments and milestones. Ryan graduated from high school on time, without any delays. For a child who had spent so much time in foster care with numerous foster home placement changes, juvenile detention, and behavior modification classes, the outcome is typically dropping out of school, never getting a GED, or spending extra years in school, past his or her eighteenth birthday, to make up lost credits. Instead, Ryan attended technical school after graduation, is gainfully employed, is in a positive relationship, and after many years has finally found his sisters.

⊨⊣⊢⊨

One more set of parents to add to the picture: **We are Mark and Sean.** We are here to share about Brian. I will save you from the suspense: we are Brian's Mama and Dad. We are OK with the titles because we know how much he loves us. We had thought about adopting for a while. Our home study had been out in the space known as the Internet for a while. Sometimes you have to take things into your own hands; this is exactly what we did. You see, each state has its own site where kids are listed when they are up for adoption. There are other sites that have listings from multiple states, like www.afamilyforeverychild.org. It may sound wrong to go on the Internet and "shop" for a child. We felt the same way at first. We tried to work with the worker assigned to our home study. It was her job to identify a child for us, which she was not doing. As we said, we were taking the search into our own hands. We didn't know what else to do. We knew that there wouldn't be an Internet site with children waiting to be adopted if there were a better way. It was pretty overwhelming to see how many children didn't have a family. It was equally overwhelming to think about why they didn't already have families. For the first time, we actually had to think about what we were getting into. We had been to the required classes and knew that kids in foster care came with scars and sometimes some really bad behaviors. We had read plenty of flyers that explained that family is needed in order for these kids to heal and learn to love. We were up for the challenge.

We sent our home study and a list of kids whom we were interested in to the Heart Gallery, website used to list children available for adoption. Before too long we got a phone call from out of state, which was fine, because it didn't matter to us where the child was from. The social worker on the other end of the phone sounded very excited to hear of our interest in Brian. She explained that she does not hold back information. She made a statement that caught us by surprise. She stated that she was going to take the process step-by-step, but if our final decision was to adopt Brian, she had a "no-return" policy. She explained that children in foster care have a lot of baggage and have experienced more rejection in their lives than we could possibly imagine. She explained that she was going to send us some documentation that would have a synopsis of Brian's history and his court report, which also goes through his history. She stated that she would wait for our phone call once we had read through the information. Afterward, we looked at each other and asked, "Does she try to push all families away? Damn— you would think that she would want to sell families on kids, not scare them away." It took us a little while to decide exactly how we wanted process of getting to know Brian to work. We wanted to know all the scary stuff; we wanted to know what we were getting into. This child was going to be ours forever, not just till age eighteen. Would we really want him introduced to us all sugarcoated?

We received a rather thick packet and started to read. The attached letter instructed us to take our time in reading through the documentation. This adorable young man that we chose online now was a real boy with lots, we mean *lots*, of baggage. How is it that one child could have lived through so much in such a short time? We continued to read, and we talked a lot. Choosing to love a child seemed like an easy decision when we started this process, but deciding to take on a child with so many scars and help him heal ended up not being so easy, at least in the beginning. We called the social worker, asked a ton of questions, and then asked the big question: Can we meet Brian? Once again the social worker tried to scare us off. "What is *with* her?" we both wondered. This time we actually asked her that question. Her response made us realize that she loves these kids so much and wants to be certain their forever families are going to love them even more. Once again she reminded me that once the Brian and we made the final decision, there was a "no-return" policy.

More questions followed, such as "Brian has to choose us too?" OK, then, let's go. "What is the next step?" Meet and greet. Arrangements were made for us to fly in and stay for a few days. We would get to spend some time with Brian and we would all get to know each other. Talk about scary! But we were so excited.

The day finally came, and we were just as excited as parents heading to a hospital to have their new baby born. There was one small difference: Our prospective new baby was fifteen years old and could actually veto us as his family. We have never heard of a newborn vetoing his parents. To say "*Wow!*" would be an understatement.

We met Brian, and we were like a family instantly. How in the world is that possible? The kid in the documentation is not who we met. We spent the entire weekend with him, and it was so hard to say good-bye. We wanted to take "our son" home.

We started talking on the phone all the time and providing for Brian in the form of financial support and gifts. We brought him out to our house, out of state, and were able to share some holidays together.

I hope that none of you think that we instantly "cured" this kid. There were still problems at school, but this time he got in trouble defending us, his dads. It felt good to know that he loved us so much that he would want to stand up for us, but he really needed to figure out better ways to handle people who pick on other people.

We became very active in our son's life. It is amazing what parents can do, even when they are several states away. There were phone conferences, team meetings, and bringing our son home on a more regular basis. (Thank heaven that our jobs provided us with free flights.) Brian learned really quickly that a trip home was not a vacation. Trouble in school came with fines and probation within the juvenile detention system, and his visits home included extra chores to earn money to pay his fines. "*Yes*, we are the parents who will hold you responsible for your actions," we would tell him. Though Brian remained in his state of origin and in his foster home, every holiday—even those little ones that equal a four-day weekend—became an opportunity to spend time together. Once again we are thankful for having jobs provide for free flights.

One small problem with having a child who lives in another state is this "wonderful" thing called the ICPC, Interstate Compact for the Placement of Children. We totally understand the reasons behind the compact, but we don't care so much for the extra time it takes to finalize an interstate adoption. It basically involves lots of paperwork—states making decisions and agreements and then seriously taking their time to respond to the adoptive parents and children. The ICPC was implemented entirely to prevent states from sending children across the country and allowing the children to drop out of the system, or be abused, neglected, or forgotten, because there wasn't a social worker checking in on them in the state they were sent to. Completing all the paperwork to get through the ICPC requirements took months, with the bottom line being that the social worker, therapist, foster parents, and his dads (that's us) fought like hell to get Brian home.

Miracle of miracles: Brian made it home, and we celebrated the adoption of our son on National Adoption Day. Our son had waited over ten years for his family. It was only fair that our special day should be a full blowout party in the court with cake, balloons, and so many people who had been part of his life all those years.

It has only been a little over a year since our family became legal. Life with Brian has not been without bumps in the road. We would like to know which home in the world with a teenager doesn't have bumps in the road. "Yes, Brian has had to go to inpatient treatment." "Yes, Brian has had a few issues with juvenile detention here." "Yes, Brian has implemented his own test." I would say that we have passed the tests: Brian came home after inpatient treatment. Brian did extra chores to pay for his new juvenile detention fines. We heard the words loud and clear, so we know that there is a no-return policy. *How do you return your son?* We wondered. Brian's aggression didn't disappear, his anger didn't vanish, and his acting out didn't evaporate into thin air the minute we signed the adoption papers. We have continued to work through these same issues for over a year now. For any of you out there thinking that we should just send him back, shame on you. You wouldn't send your child back to where he or she came from.

Our son may have been adopted and by some crazy definition have a "system" to go back to, and your child may no longer fit back in the space he or she came from, but they are both children. We would not send our son back any sooner than you would try to put yours back into a very small birth canal. We continue to love him through the "yuk" and rejoice in the positives. For example, Brian was just promoted to tenth grade. He struggles with math and science but participates in tutorials and is doing great.

We love him too much to ever think about letting someone else travel this road with him. Besides, it was passing Brian's test that has made the difference in his life and in ours. We can tell you that our son has made friends, is excelling in school, and has been the best part of the addition to our family. Brian didn't just gain a dad and a dad, one of whom he refers to as "Mama," but he gained aunts, uncles, grandparents, and cousins. He always seems a little overwhelmed that so many people can love him so much—but *we do*, and now he knows it!

⥤⥢ ⥤⥢

CHAPTER 4
APRIL AND ANNIE

My name is April, and this is my baby sister, Annie. We live with our mommy and daddy. Daddy goes to work every day, and Mommy takes care of Annie and me. Mommy takes us to go shopping with her and always lets us pick out something special. I always pick out Oreos, and Annie loves juice in a box. Mommy takes us to the park a lot, and sometimes when it gets really hot out, we get to go to the pool. After the park or pool, we always go home and get a snack and then a nap. I think that I am too old for naps, but for some reason I seem to always fall asleep. I guess that it is OK, though, because I always get up before Annie, so I get to choose what to watch on TV and don't have to share with Annie. Since she is the baby, she always gets to choose what to watch when she wakes up.

Daddy comes home, and then we eat dinner as a family. I like it when Daddy gets home. He plays with Annie and me. Sometimes we play a game or just color together. I love coloring. I think that Daddy must bring us new coloring books every day because he really wants to color. I don't know about other daddies, but our daddy likes to color.

Today Daddy came home from work before we got home from the park. Annie and I were so excited and ran to get our colors. When we came out from our bedroom, Mommy and Daddy were yelling at each other. I don't know that Annie and me have ever heard them yell at each other or us. But today was weird; they did both. When we came running into the kitchen with our colors and books, Mommy yelled that we needed to go back to our room. I took Annie's hand and walked her to our room. I gave her the colors and books, and she colored on her bed. I sat next to my door and just listened to Mommy and Daddy. I don't think they have ever been so mad at each other. Mommy said that Daddy had been lying. Annie and me are not allowed to lie, and neither should Daddy. Daddy said something about Mommy not complaining when she had lots of money to go shopping with. Mommy kept yelling and using really bad words. She said that there wouldn't be any money if he got caught doing it. I thought that you always got money when you go to work. I am very confused.

Mommy and Daddy are still fighting, and a policeman comes to our house. He takes Daddy with him. I don't know where they are going. Mommy tries to explain to Annie and me that Daddy has been bad and he wasn't working like he was supposed to be. She said she was very sorry, but Daddy wasn't going to be coming home for a very long time. I tried to ask Mommy where he was going. She just said he got himself "locked up."

Mommy hasn't taken us shopping in a long time. We haven't gone to the park or the pool. Mommy cries a lot. Grandma brought us some food, and I have learned how to cook for Annie and me. Well, I can't cook like Mommy used to, but I can use the microwave.

Mommy tucked us in bed tonight. She said that we needed to make sure that we went potty because once she locked our door we would have to wait till morning before we could go again. I took Annie again and told her to try again. We both tried to pee again since Mommy seemed really mad at us. We went to bed and made sure not to come out of our room.

I think Mommy has a new boyfriend since Daddy hasn't come home in a long time. He only comes over to see her when we go to bed. He has never colored with us like Daddy used to. He hasn't had dinner with us either. He is always gone before we get up in the morning. Mommy and her new boyfriend usually see each other in Mommy's room. I don't know what they are doing, but they pound on the wall a lot. I don't think that it is with their fists. It kind of sounds like when Annie and me jump on our beds. We are not allowed to jump on our beds, so I didn't know that Mommy was allowed to. Maybe her new boyfriend is allowed to jump on the bed. It is really loud and scares Annie, so she comes and sleeps in my bed with me. My bed is not up against Mommy's room, so it is not as loud on my side of the room. I tell Annie they are just playing and having fun and it will make Mommy happy again and we will be able to go shopping together, and to the park and to the pool again.

Mommy puts us to bed as usual. Tonight I think she has a new boyfriend. He doesn't have the same voice as the other guy. We never got to meet the other boyfriend, so I guess it doesn't matter if she has a new one. This boyfriend likes to jump on the bed with Mommy also, but he yells when he jumps. He is weird. Annie sleeps with me all the time now. I wonder if we will get to meet this boyfriend. I wonder if this boyfriend will color with us or make Mommy happy like she used to be. He wasn't here in the morning when we got up, so I guess not.

Before we went to bed tonight, Mommy introduced us to our new daddy. I don't know why we need a new daddy. I like our other daddy and just want him to come home so that things can be like they used to be. Mommy said he was never coming home and our new daddy was better and made her very happy. She doesn't look happy, but she doesn't like lying so she must be. Mommy tucks us in bed and locks the door. I really don't like this daddy. Our other daddy never made us lock our door at night.

Mommy had a friend come visit. He can't be her boyfriend 'cause she has our new Daddy. Her new friend jumps on her bed while Daddy watches TV in the living room. I am used to the noise that the bed makes when you jump on it and don't have any trouble sleeping anymore. I woke up all of a sudden tonight. The noise wasn't from Mommy's friends jumping on the bed, but Mommy and the new daddy were yelling at each other. I went and sat next to my door so I could hear better. Daddy was telling Mommy that she could have more money if she let him pimp Annie and me. I don't know what that means. I guess it doesn't matter 'cause Mommy was yelling at him and saying "NO." Mommy said that he could pimp her all day long and give her whatever he needed to, to keep her awake and making everyone happy. She kept yelling that Annie and me were not to be touched.

I woke up before Annie this morning. I am so glad she didn't get woken up by all the yelling last night. She has learned to block out a lot of noises since our first daddy got taken away by the policeman. Mommy never unlocked our door like she usually does. I unlocked it from my side even though I am not supposed to. The house was quiet, and I really had to pee, so I figured it would be OK. I tiptoed out of my room and didn't see anyone in the living room. I ran to the bathroom so that I could get back in my room before anyone knew I was out. I didn't want to get in trouble. Mommy's bedroom door was open, so I peeked my head in to see if she was awake. Mommy was sitting on the side of her bed. She must be sick. I sat quiet next to her door as she put a belt around her arm real tight and then took a needle with medicine she had heated up in a spoon and stuck it into her arm. Annie and me have gotten shots before, but our doctor never had to warm it up. Grown-ups must get different stuff than kids. I didn't say a word. I felt bad that Mommy was sick. I turned and went back to my room but made sure not to make any noise.

Mommy has been really, really sick. She takes a lot of medicine but is still able to visit with her friends at night and must feel better at night 'cause she still has energy to jump on her bed. Mommy seems to have a lot of friends lately. I don't even know how many different voices were in the house last night.

Annie and I got up and waited for Mommy to get up. She wouldn't wake up, so I took Annie with me into the kitchen to find something to eat. I could only find the noodles in the square plastic. I put them in a bowl with water and the little packets of powder that make it taste better. I never know how long it is supposed to be in the microwave, so I always push the buttons of my age. I turned six before Daddy got taken by the policeman, so I put 6-0-0 into the microwave. Our new daddy came into the kitchen and started treating Annie very special. He was playing with her hair and talking really nice to her. He told her how pretty she was. Mommy finally woke up and came into the kitchen. She was so mad at Daddy and told him to take his hands off Annie. She was yelling at him really, really loud. I tried to move Annie out of their way by grabbing her hand. I couldn't reach her. The microwave beeped, and I tried to ask Mommy if I could take Annie and the noodles to the table to eat. Our new daddy was so mad. He grabbed the noodles out of the microwave and threw them at Annie and Mommy. The noodles hit Annie in the face and fell on her shoulder and arm. It is always so hot when it comes out of the microwave. I have to let it cool. It must have really hurt. Annie was crying so loud I started to cry with her. Mommy and Daddy just kept yelling. I grabbed Annie and ran to our room. I grabbed Daddy's new phone and locked our door. I don't know any phone numbers. What am I going to do with the phone? Annie is still crying, and her face looks like she had fire, not noodles, put on her. I remember when we used to go to the pool there were signs that had the number 911 if someone was hurt. I didn't know any other numbers so I pushed the 911. A very nice lade answered the phone. She asked how she could help me. I told her that my Mommy and my new Daddy were fighting and that Annie got noodles spilled on her and her face looked like fire and she won't stop crying. The nice lady asked if I knew my address. I started crying and told her, "No." She told me not to cry, that she could find me anyway. She told me to stay on the phone. She asked if Annie and me were in a safe place now. I told her I had taken Annie into our room and locked the door. She told me I was a brave girl and she was very proud of me for remembering the phone number to call when someone is hurt. She told me people would be coming real soon to help Annie and me. She told me there would be an ambulance that would take Annie and me to the doctor and a policeman so Mommy and my new daddy would stop fighting. The nice lady on the other side of the phone stayed on the phone talking to me until the other people showed up. When the ambulance showed up, the nice lady told me that it was OK to unlock the door for them. She reminded me how brave I was and how proud of me she was. She told me that I could hang up now so I did.

The lady and man in the ambulance came in after the policeman moved Mommy and Daddy to their room. They came to Annie and me and started talking to us and looking at Annie. They took off all the noodles very carefully and put some medicine on her face, shoulder, and arm, and then they put some big Band-Aids on her. We both got to take a ride in the ambulance to the doctors. They even put on those special lights and sirens. That was pretty cool. Annie has stopped crying, but I am sure that it still hurts. The lady on the phone should have told Annie she was brave too. I told Annie that she was very brave. The lady in the ambulance with us told Annie that I was right; she was the bravest little girl she has ever met. We got to the hospital, but Mommy and Daddy didn't come. The doctor said that they were talking to the policeman and would come to see us soon. Instead of Mommy, a different lady came to talk to us. Annie wouldn't talk to her, so I did. She asked me a lot of questions. She asked about the noodles, Mommy's medicine, Mommy's friends, and our new daddy. She explained that we were going to go visit some friends of hers for a few days so that we could rest and Annie could get better.

We must have driven forever. These friends lived very far from our house. I am not sure where it is, but they better remember how to get back home. Mommy is going to wonder where we are. Well, maybe she doesn't care where we are. It has been over a week, and we haven't even talked to her.

I got to go to school for the first time, and Mommy didn't even come and take my picture like she used to say she was going to do. That is probably because that was before Daddy left and all of her boyfriends started coming over. That was before our new daddy, and before Mommy started taking medicine with the needles.

We didn't have to go to school today. Well, I didn't go to school. Annie actually goes to day care, but she thinks it is her school. The family that we are living with said that we were going to see our mommy. I am so excited. I started to pack my clothes in a bag and had started putting Annie's clothes in a bag when the mother came into our room and said we were not leaving; we were just going to visit Mommy, and then we would be coming back to her house. She tried to explain they were foster parents and take care of kids when their mommies and daddies are sick or need help taking care of their kids. I guess that makes sense since I know Mommy has been taking a lot of medicine.

We drove for a very long time and finally got to a building with lots of people and the lady we now know as our caseworker. She explained that she gets to see us and is helping Mommy so we can hopefully go home as soon as possible. She said it was up to Mommy to get better. We were taken into this room that had a bunch of toys. We were in there forever. Mommy finally showed up.

Annie and me hugged her, and we were all crying. I told Mommy that she needed to get better really soon so that we could go home. She said that she was working on it, though she said she was not as sick as the caseworker said she was. I told her the caseworker didn't say she was very sick. Mommy promised we would be coming home in a few days. I told Mommy that the caseworker didn't say we would go home that soon and it was up to Mommy to work at feeling better. I told Mommy she didn't look better. She yelled at me and said I had no clue what I was talking about. She kept yelling like when we were at home and she didn't have any medicine to take. I told Mommy she should ask the caseworker to get her some medicine so she would feel better. Mommy said she doesn't take any medicine. I really don't understand. I have seen the needles.

It is almost Thanksgiving break at school. We go to see Mommy every week on Wednesday. Annie and I never miss going, not even once. Mommy sometimes is there, but most of the time she doesn't come to see us. I am very mad at her. If she doesn't care to see us, I don't even want her to be our mommy anymore. We got a new daddy when the first one left and then the second one left. We had one foster mother and foster father, and then we left them. I don't know why all the mommies and daddies are allowed to leave us behind. When our first daddy and mommy were together before the policeman took him away, we got to go shopping, got to go to the park, got to color with Daddy, and all sorts of nice stuff. The policeman never should have taken Daddy.

Annie and me were talking, and we decided that if all these mommies and daddies are allowed to leave whenever they want, then we can too. We can't drive, and a lot of these homes are way far away. Annie broke a lot of toys at the last house, so maybe if we break all the mommies' and daddies' toys, we can leave them. That worked at the first two houses but not the third. I decided to break the house. You can actually kick some doors so that your foot goes right through them. It kind of hurts, but when you are mad at everyone, it really doesn't bother me anymore. I broke two doors now, Annie broke all the toys, and we both jumped so hard on the bed that it broke too. This mommy and daddy said that they loved us anyway. I think it is because they go to church a lot. Maybe they think that God is going to fix us. This daddy has to talk all the time at the front of the church. He was talking about loving people no matter what. I wonder if that means Annie and me. Maybe our first mommy and daddy should have come here, and then they would have known that they shouldn't leave and stop loving us.

I told Annie that we should stop breaking things 'cause this mommy and daddy are going to love us no matter what. That means that they won't leave. I like this mommy and daddy. When I see my first mommy again, I am going to tell her she doesn't need to come back 'cause we have a new mommy and daddy. I guess she actually needs to come and see us or I can't tell her. It has been a long time since she came to the office with all the toys to see us.

The caseworker came to see us today. She sat down with Mommy, Daddy, Annie, and me. She told us that Daddy is a pastor, which means that he is the one that gets to talk at the front of the church. She explained that sometimes there are people who are like his boss, and they make daddies go to new churches to talk to people who don't know you have to love people no matter what. Sometimes when the bosses send daddies to these new places, they don't understand they have children that can't go with them. I told her that Annie and me would go wherever Mommy and Daddy went. She tried to explain there is a judge who makes all the decisions as to where we are allowed to live and he said "no." I told the caseworker that I needed to tell him we need to go with our mommy and daddy. She said he wants us to go home to our first mommy when she feels better. I told her that she is not our mommy anymore 'cause she doesn't even come to see us. Our new mommy and daddy were crying, and Annie and me were crying.

This is *stupid*. This stupid judge hasn't even met Annie or me. How does he know who our mommy and daddy should be? The caseworker tried again to help us understand. She asked if we knew what laws were—like cars have to stop at stop signs, you can't take stuff from the store without giving them money, and stuff like that? Annie and me said, "Yes." She said there are laws about first mommies and daddies and their kids. The law says the judge has to give the kids back to their first mommies and daddies if they get better and do everything the judge says. I asked if Mommy has done everything she was told to do. The caseworker said not yet, but the judge gives her a whole year to do it. She explained that part of what Mommy had to do is have a chance to see Annie and me once a week. I told the caseworker she never comes anyway, so we shouldn't have to go. She said she knew what we were saying, but the judge said we still have to try. She explained if we moved far, far away, then we wouldn't be able to come and see her if she showed up. This is why we aren't allowed to move with our new mommy and daddy. We just cried. Annie and me didn't know what else to do. Grown-ups, like judges, are obviously allowed to do what they want as long as the law says they can.

I asked the caseworker what happens when our first mommy and daddy's year is up and the law is done. She said that the judge would then decide if we can have a new mommy and daddy who would love us forever. I told her I want the year to be over. She reminded me that we went to our first foster home when school started, so when it is time for school to start again it will be close to that time. She told me she would let me know when the judge makes up his mind if we can have a new mommy and daddy or not. She said if this is what happens, she will sit down with Annie and me and explain everything, but for today she needed to find us a new mommy and daddy until the judge makes up his mind. She told us they probably would just be our mommy and daddy for a little time. We said that was OK as long as she kept coming over to tell us what we were going to do next. She promised that as long as she was our caseworker, she would always tell us the truth and explain things the best that she could. She made us promise that we would ask questions if we didn't understand and be good at the new foster home because they were just trying to help us until the judge said what he was going to make us do. I asked her why the other caseworker didn't tell us what was going on. She said that all caseworkers don't think kids will understand, so they don't explain stuff. I told her they should at least try. "Kids aren't stupid." She agreed with me.

The caseworker came and took us to our new foster home. She reminded us this was just temporary and we should listen to the mom and dad and follow the rules of the home. Annie and me agreed that we would. I asked if we would still be able to go to church even though our last daddy no longer talked there. She said she would request that the new mom and dad take us, but with the other children in the home, this may not always be possible. The caseworker said she would talk to the other daddy to see if there was someone from the church who might be able to pick us up and take us since the church was close to our new home. I told her there was this really nice lady who did the kids' school at church. The caseworker said she would call her.

Our caseworker talked to Sue, and she agreed to pick us up. Our caseworker explained [that] everyone who drove us around or took care of us had to have permission, but since she took care of kids at church, she already had this kind of permission, so she could start right away. Annie and me were very excited. Finally we got to keep something. We didn't have the same mommy and daddy anymore, but we still got to go to the church that we called ours, and we got to see Sue and all our friends at church.

Sue picked us up this morning for church. We were so happy to see everyone even though our other daddy was gone. Sue introduced us to new friends and a new family that said that they would like Annie and me to think about coming to stay with them. They said if the judge said they could have a new mommy and daddy that would be ours forever, they would really like to be them. They have a daughter who is a year older than me. I like her a lot, and we hang out all the time at church. We always sit next to each other. We even get to go to lunch after church with them as long as Sue comes with us. I guess that is because she already had permission. (Sue told us that even though she is much older, this family is actually her mom, dad, and sister.) Sue agreed that if the judge gives us permission to have a new mommy and daddy forever, she would love to have two new sisters.

Annie and me asked our caseworker if Sue's family could be our family forever. She explained she was going to see the judge next week, and he was going to make up his mind if we were going to get a new mommy and daddy to keep forever. She said just in case he did, she was going to have Sue's family get special permission to let us be in their family. The caseworker explained that sometimes this permission takes a lot of time to get. I asked what they had to do and told her I would help. I showed her I was learning to write and could write a letter so they could get permission right away. She explained there is a special school for people who want to be a kid's family when they are not their first mommy and daddy. I told her that maybe my first mommy and daddy should have taken the class and then they would not have left us behind. She explained that unfortunately that is not how things work. I told her they really should.

The caseworker came to visit today. She sat with Annie and me. She looked very serious, which was really scary. She had Sue and her family visit with us. She explained the judge said that our first mommy and daddy were no longer going to be our parents and he was no longer going to try and send us back to them. The caseworker said their rights had been terminated. She said this means they can't have us back, ever. She explained that even though they couldn't have us back, they would get a chance to say good-bye if they wanted to show up. She explained this would be the last time Annie and me would have to go to her office with all the toys to see our first mommy. Annie and me said we didn't want to say good-bye, but she explained that once more the judge said we had to go, but only once. This meant if she didn't show up, we never had to go back. I told Annie we could go one more time; it would be OK.

We went to the office today. Our first mommy actually came this time. She cried a lot. She brought all these toys for us to keep. Our caseworker sat in the room with us. I heard her tell Mommy she needed to try not to cry and to enjoy her time with us and not to make any promises or the visit would be stopped. We sat and played for a little while, and then Mommy told us that she was going to fight hard and we would be going home with her really soon. The caseworker reminded her not to make promises. Mommy started yelling at her, telling her that she would say what she wanted to because we were her daughters and we needed to know she wasn't done fighting. Our caseworker told her if she continued, the visit would be over. I really wanted her to keep yelling so we could leave. She stopped for a little while and then started promising us again. The caseworker said that was enough and one more comment would end the visit. She stepped to the door and asked for a boss to come to the door. Mommy started yelling and saying really bad words. The boss lady took Mommy by the arm and walked her out of the room. Our caseworker came over to us and said she was very sorry, but our first mommy would not be coming back because she was not listening and following the rules like the judge had told her too. I told the caseworker I wanted her to leave anyway. I didn't want to see her since she didn't want to see us all this time. Our caseworker walked us to a back door, where our foster mom was waiting for us. This was not the same door we came in, but I guess that is because our mommy was at the other door. We could still hear her yelling. When we drove away, there was a policeman putting her in the car. I guess she gets to go be with our first daddy. At least they have each other; Annie and me have each other; seems fair to me.

⇥ ⇤

We are Donna and Derik, soon to be the family for Annie and April. We have been going to church with the girls for quite a while now. We have never thought about adopting before, especially children that have been in foster care. We even gave this a second thought and a lot of prayer when we found out how much goes into being adoptive parents. It isn't just picking out a couple of kids and calling them ours. It isn't setting up beds, getting them registered in a new school, or just going to court. It is a complete home study. This in and of itself is not even that simple. There are a ton of questions about every aspect of our lives: finances, other children, extended family and how they feel about us adopting, if we drink or smoke, if we ever had marital problems, references...On top of the laundry list of questions and answers, there is the actual house preparation—yes, new beds and dressers, but also things that my own biological children have lived without: a specified number of fire extinguishers, smoke detectors, CO_2 sensors, fire escape ladders on the second floor, proof of income, and parenting classes as well as first-aid and CPR training. In the back of my head, all I could think was that if all parents had to go through this much work before having a child, we wouldn't need a child welfare system. Regardless of all the work, April and Annie are well worth every step.

Every question got answered, every class completed, and every required item purchased and installed as well as checked for safety. After all of that, our home study was complete, and the powers that be had to review it to decide if we were a good match for two girls we already considered our own. What would we do if they said no? I wouldn't have the strength to tell them we couldn't be their mommy and daddy. Surely these powers wouldn't do such a thing. Thank God, the girls' caseworker fought hard, and we were approved.

The day had come. Our daughters were coming home. No longer would they be shuffled around. No longer would they have to start yet another new school or new church, or leave their friends just to have to try and make new ones. Finally, they would have the one mommy and daddy God had intended for them all along.

My husband and I have realized that in life, there are quite a few steps, stumbles, and trials that have to be taken or overcome to end up where you belong. April and Annie were always supposed to be our daughters. This was God's plan all along. It is the many families, schools, and friends they have gone through who make them who they are and make them the kids that we love so much. We wouldn't want it any other way. It would have been nice to protect them from any pain and every tear, but then they never would have become the amazingly strong young ladies they are. They never would have acquired the voices they have to share their story and be support to so many other children that come and go within their school, church and neighborhood.

CHAPTER 5
JUSTIN AND SIBLINGS

My name is Justin, and I have four brothers and sisters. Kevin is four years older than me, and Heather is two years older. Then there is Amanda; she came after me—by two years. And last is Seth. He is the baby, and we all make sure he is taken care of. Actually, Kevin looks out for all of us, kind of like a dad.

My family is like every other family. We don't have much money and live in a small house. Mom and Dad have a bed; Kevin, Seth, and me have a bed; and Heather and Amanda have a bed. When it is cold out, we usually all sleep in one bed. There are times when Seth is scared and he will jump in whatever bed he wants, which is OK 'cause he is Seth. We eat breakfast and lunch at school with all the other kids. I like the days that we get to go to school, not 'cause I like school but 'cause that is where they keep the food; kinda weird that food is only at a place that kids don't like to go. Mom and Dad must have their own school they go to.

There is this lady that comes to our house when we don't go to school. Sometimes she comes more in the summer and around Christmas when we can't go to school. We all think she is a special lady 'cause we hurry and clean the house when we see her driving through the parking lot. When the windows are open, you can hear her tires on the gravel. When the windows are closed, we just don't open the door for her until we clean up a little. We don't like to clean, but we are really fast when she comes to visit. I'm not sure why, but we see the doctor every time she visits, and we are allowed to have food in the house for a little while after she leaves. She likes to come see us a couple times in a row to look at our food and see the doctor papers. I don't know why she would want to look at food that she never eats. When I go somewhere that gots food, I always ask if they will share. My friends must not know that food is only allowed at school.

Seth was really sick once, and the special lady had Mom take him to the doctor. I don't think it was real bad 'cause he didn't have to go back. Mom got sick once, and she got to go to the doctor a whole lot of times. It didn't make much sense since she just got sicker and sicker every time she went. I decided that I didn't mind not going to the doctor when I was sick 'cause it only makes it worse. The doctors must be really bad 'cause Mom won't even get out of bed anymore and has stopped going to see them. I don't really understand, and Dad said it is none of our business.

The other day the ambulance came and took Mom to the doctor. She was gone for a while. Dad said it was still none of our business. I guess the special lady must have sent the ambulance to pick her up 'cause she was the one who always made us kids go to the doctor. Mom has been gone for over a week, and today Dad said she was never coming back. Our grandma came to drive us to this place. Mom was sleeping in a box. Dad thinks if he doesn't say anything, then we won't know what is going on. Kevin told us kids that Mom had died and Jesus took her to heaven. It isn't fair. He should have taken all of us to heaven. We are a family, and family stays together. Everyone was crying a lot. I didn't cry, not sure why.

Things are really weird now that Mom is gone. Dad sits all day, and Kevin takes care of us all the time. He doesn't make us go to school at all like Mom sometimes did. I asked if I could go to have some food. Kevin said no, but he took some of Dad's money and brought some food home. Now that Mom is gone, Dad has money even when he just sits. He doesn't even have to work. I want to have that someday. Maybe if Mom had gone to heaven sooner, we would have been allowed to have food in the house all the time. I really don't know how that works.

A police car came to our house today along with the special lady. The police didn't give us any time to clean before we opened the door. I think that this made the lady mad 'cause she took all us kids away from our dad. He went with the police. Maybe if we had cleaned the house, the police wouldn't have taken Dad away. I don't know where Kevin and my sisters went. Seth and I stayed with these people we didn't know. They were OK, I guess. They gave us food and two separate beds. Me and Seth figured we would share a bed like at home so some other kids could have the one Seth wasn't using. We sleep in one bed anyway, so there is no reason to waste the other one.

We all got taken to talk to these people. They asked all sorts of questions: where we sleep; what we ate for breakfast, lunch, and dinner; what we call different parts of our bodies; and if anyone has touched us. Kevin already told us that family stuff is not to be talked about, so I didn't say anything. I am sure that Seth and the girls said nothing either. We always listen to Kevin. He is the oldest and knows best. Someone said Dad had touched a girl, and it was OK to say if he had touched us. We don't talk about stuff like that. I didn't say anything.

The lady asked Dad if there was family or friends that all of us kids could stay with. I guess he asked a whole bunch of Mom's brothers and sisters, but they must have said no. Maybe when Mom went to heaven that meant they were not our aunts and uncles anymore. Grandma had to say no 'cause her house is so small. She has these friends, though, who said we could stay with them, so that is where we went. I don't really like them, but at least we all get to be together. We were all told we have to have our own beds and we are not allowed to share. I wasn't going to ask if it was OK for Seth to still sleep where he wanted or if when one of us was scared or cold, we were allow to share.

Kevin asked when Dad was coming back because he isn't going to stay here. The lady tried to explain that Dad had been bad and was going away for a very long time. Kevin explained to the rest of us kids that the police and the lady were all liars and were saying that Dad touched a girl's tinkle. None of us believe them, and they shouldn't be lying about stuff.

They told us that these ladies who keep coming to visit are actually social workers and seem to have all the power. We haven't seen or talked to our dad in a long time. The social worker said that the judge said he couldn't have any contact with us or any other kids because of what he did to the other little girl. The judge must have listened to what Kevin says are all lies and actually believed it. This is so confusing to me and especially Seth.

I don't really like these family friends of Grandma's. They are really mean. They don't hit or anything, but they always seem mad, yell about school and how I read, and keep telling me to stop looking at people "that way." I don't know what they are talking about—how I look at people. My reading is really bad, and I have to play with books to see the words. They think that I am goofing around, but I really am not. I do have to say they always have a lot of food in the house. We get to eat dinner and have to eat together. We still run around and clean really quick when the social worker shows up. That is what we have always done.

Seth had a really bad day today, so I ran in our room and jumped on top of him and kissed him. Carl, the husband of Grandma's friend that we are living with, came in the room and got really, really mad. He called our social worker, who came out, and all of a sudden I was moved to a new home without any of my brothers or sisters. Someone needs to explain this. I heard the social worker and the new family talking in the other room. She said something about sexually acting out. What is she talking about? From then on I had to go and talk to this guy who said he was a therapist. He kept asking lots of questions about being touched and touching others. I just sit quiet. This is a total waste of my time, so I will waste his time.

Today I was told that the family that I was staying with was just temporary, for emergencies only. I don't know what the emergency was. Seth and I weren't doing anything wrong. Either way, I had to go to another family. They are nice enough and try to talk to me all the time. I am here all by myself and really wish that I could be with my brothers and sisters. The social worker told me that she is working on it, but I don't know what that means. I do get to see them once a week at church and sometimes twice if I get to go on Wednesday, but this is not the same as living with them. No one will tell me when we will all be together again. When I see Kevin at church, he tells me to be strong and he will have us all together again soon. He reminds me that he promised Dad he would take care of us, so that is what he is going to do. I believe him. Kevin has always done what he is told and would not go back on his word to Dad.

I am not sure why this new family cares so much, but they seem to. I have gone to the doctor a whole bunch. I haven't felt sick, but the mother says they are trying to figure out why I have trouble reading and make funny faces at people. Today I got to see a special eye doctor. Oh, I hope that I don't need glasses. I will definitely be made fun of if I have to wear glasses. But the doctor says I don't need any. *Yay, no glasses.* I do, however, have to go to this therapy. I hope they don't think that I am actually going to talk to someone. I didn't last time. Well, it is not that kind of therapy. I go see the eye doctor once a week and we play these games. The doctor tried to explain to me that I have this really big word: "eye convergence." Basically, my eyes never got the right muscles when I was little, so I have a hard time seeing words on paper. She explained that steering the book in front of me like a steering wheel helps me focus. She says the exercises will help make my eyes strong. The exercises are actually like games on the computer, so I don't mind doing them.

"More doctors?" I ask. This time it is to figure out why I make funny faces. To tell you the truth, I have no idea what they are talking about. Now the new doctor is trying to explain yet another thing wrong with me. I don't know why I am going to try and explain it to you 'cause it makes no sense to me. It is called Tourette's syndrome. This doesn't get games to fix it like my eyes. Now I have to take these pills. I don't like them; they make me feel funny. I take them, though, 'cause I don't want this family mad at me and make me move again.

As if things weren't bad enough, I got a new social worker. She came to see me tonight. Little does she know that I don't talk to social workers. It is usually a quick five-minute visit 'cause they get fed up with me. She meets with the foster parents first. I really don't care what they have to say. She finally comes and knocks at my door. She tells me her name and starts talking about the pictures on my walls. I don't bother to respond and just start shooting hoops with the balls and closet door hoop. She grabs the ball and asks if she can try. I am not going to talk to her anyway, so just shrug my shoulders. She is really bad and misses completely. I can't help but laugh at her. She laughs too and asks me to show her how it is done. I shoot and swish right in. She compliments my shot and tries again. This time she makes it and I have to compliment her. She just smiles. Then she sees the toys on my desk. She asks who the characters are.

"*Seriously?*" How can she not know who Alex the Lion and Melman are?

"*Really?*" She has no clue who the *Ice Age* characters are either.

I have to ask, "Haven't you seen anything?"

She admits that she has not seen *Ice Age* or *Madagascar*—any of them! I decide to tell her that she is not allowed to come back unless she sees all of them.

She comes back with, "OK, but if I see all of them and can actually talk about them, then you have to talk to me about something I want." I agree to her demands. I know she is a social worker and will never do as she says anyway, so I will not have to worry about talking about anything that I don't want.

A month has passed since I last saw the social worker. Eye therapy is OK and school is easier. I actually read a real book, *crazy!* I am taking my meds as I am told and must admit that I feel a little better with them as well. The social worker is back. She knocks on my door again and comes in. I start in immediately with questions and answers about the movies. She asks if we can do question for question. I respond that for every two correct answers from her I will answer one question. She agrees. So I have to.

She knows all the guys in *Ice Age*; I tell her about the book I read. She knows all the guys from *Madagascar*; I tell her about therapy. She knows where Alex and the gang have been; I tell her the last time I saw my siblings. Somewhere along the way we went from questions and answers to just talking. I am kind of shocked that she actually just sits and talks to me. The foster dad comes in and says he hates to interrupt, but it is getting late and I have to get ready for bed. *Wow,* I have never had a social worker just sit and talk to me for so long. I ask her when she is coming back, and she actually sets a date in her book and writes my name down. I feel important being in her book. I kind of liked today's game, so told her she had to know who danced and got voted off *Dancing with the Stars* if she expected to talk to me next time. *Na, take that,* I thought; she'd never get it right.

She's *baaaack.* Of course she is prepared with answers about *Dancing with the Stars* and *baaaam,* she even knows that *Madagascar* is having a Christmas special. You guessed it; this meant serious conversations. Today we talked about the fact that the court said we could never go back with our dad 'cause he got sent to prison for a long time. She explained she wanted me to be with a family forever and not keep moving to new foster homes. The only response I could think of was "Will my brothers and sisters come?" She said that is what she wanted for me but wasn't going to promise something until she could back it up. Once again, I am a little shocked. I was expecting "I'll get back to you" or a promise that will never come true. She asks if I would come with her to have some pictures taken, and then she explained they would be with my siblings who want to come.

I asked, "Why not all of them?" She said that Kevin and Heather are refusing to be adopted, and due to their ages, it is their choices. She explained that Amanda really wants to be adopted by Grandma's friends, so it most likely would just be Seth and I. She did say that the plan would be to keep talking to all the brothers and sisters, but if they didn't change their minds, then she would keep Seth and me together, making sure that whatever family was found would agree to let us visit each other. I guess I don't have much else to say. We schedule a date and time for pictures. Once again I am in her book.

Seth and I get our pictures taken. That was fun. And we got ice cream out of it. A few weeks later we got to go up the Space Needle and had a video taken. We got presents from the tour guides. It was actually kind of fun, and for a while I forgot that this was all about finding a new family for Seth and me. We were just having fun spending the day together.

I can tell you that I met this man who might become my new dad, but I think that he tells the story of how we met better than I can. This is my dad, Chase.

I am Chase. I am a single adult male and came out of the closet a long time ago. I have decided I want nothing more in life than to have a family of my own. I have discussed this with my parents and siblings. As always, they are all very supportive. I took the first step to find the children God intended to be my family. The first step is to complete the home study process. This is a time-consuming process: background checks, questions about every part of my life, classes about adoption and children in foster care, home inspections, and safety upgrades. If I had any ideas about being private or protecting personal details of my life, I had to put that all aside in order to have a family. All I could think is that maybe there would be a lot less children in foster care waiting to be adopted if all parents had to go through the scrutiny I did.

Once my home study was complete, there were more choices to be made. I could look for children on the numerous websites that list children who are free for adoption. I could have my home study worker search for children within my parameters. I could have my home study added to other websites that list families looking to adopt. Or I could go all out and do all of the above. You guessed it, the chances are better if I do all of the above. My home study was put out "there," and my worker and I went to work looking at the never-ending list of children looking for a family. I really didn't think my home study would get pulled off the website, but it couldn't hurt. There is that small possibility that a social worker may actually check the website and select me as a possible family for children he or she is working with.

I found out there are all sorts of people working to find children their forever homes. The children have a social worker. Some children have a special adoption recruiter looking for families. Of course, I had my own worker. I got a call that a social worker for two boys had read my home study and was requesting that I consider her children. These children had a special recruiter from Wendy's Wonderful Kids (Dave Thomas Foundation for

Adoption). The recruiter provided me a packet of information to review that gave me more details than I had expected about these kids. As I read, I was seriously overwhelmed. These boys were also much older than I was willing to consider. I passed on the word that my answer was no. Besides, I had already requested to be considered for another child. The child had several families interested in him, so they were holding a selection committee to make a decision. I was so excited; I knew I had a good chance of being selected. But then my heart was broken: I was not chosen. Someone thought I was not a good match for the boy who I felt so strongly was mine.

I don't think even a day passed before I got another call from my worker. She explained that the social worker of the two boys who I had already read about had not given up. She stated that the social worker and the special recruiter knew I had not been chosen for the other child and were simply requesting to meet me in person to answer any questions that I might have. I informed her that I had already said no because they were too old. She stated the children's social worker was very persistent and simply wanted one meeting, and then I could give a solid no. Well, if this is the only way to get this woman to stop stalking me, it wouldn't hurt. It was only an hour out of my day, and she was even going to come to my house so I didn't have to waste my time driving somewhere.

In preparation for the meeting, I reread the documents I had already received. I made myself a long list of questions in the hopes of scaring this crazy stalker person away. I already had my mind made up, so it was her time she was wasting. The social worker and the special recruiter arrived on time. I didn't expect any less. I started with my firm belief that the boys who they were here about were way too old to be the children I was looking to adopt. The social worker turned to me and just about knocked me off my chair.

She asked, "When did your parents stop being your parents? Was it at the age of eighteen? Have you relied more on your parents as an adult or a minor child?" Of course my parents didn't throw me aside on my eighteenth birthday. They have supported me throughout my life.

Then she continued with the questions. "Do you plan on no longer being the father of the children you adopt on their eighteenth birthday?"

"Of course not!" I had to have a strong comeback to this. My response was: "I want to have more time getting to know them, so I want to start out young."

Once again a smart-ass response: "How much did your parents know about you when you were young? Did having you since you were born make it so they knew you better?"

"*Wow!*" I was speechless. Deep inside I knew that my parents knew very little about me when I was younger. There were many secrets I kept for a long time. Being born to my parents had nothing to do with how much they knew about me or how much I allowed them to know.

Do her comments never end? I wondered. "You have the luxury of having a complete family history, court reports, department documentation, doctor reports, etc., at your fingertips. You will have more information about these two boys than your parents started with or even discovered by your eighteenth birthday."

OK, all these were good points. This is still a lot to take in. I was hopeful that this was the end of this meeting, but from what I have seen of this social worker, it was far from over.

Then she asked the question that I didn't want to even consider: "How about a simple play date?"

"What does that mean?" I countered.

She explained she would plan a date for the boys and me. She would explain to the boys that I was just a friend who wanted to go bowling with them. Bowling allows for an activity to keep everyone occupied and not just staring at each other over a meal. If all goes well, dinner could follow. She stated that we would take it from there. If my answer was still a solid *no*, she would stop stalking me. I agreed to bowling.

Before leaving, she made one more comment that left my head spinning. She said, "I read your home study cover to cover and know you are a strong Christian, as am I. I pray for my children every night. When I read your home study, there was a peace that I cannot explain, but I knew God had set your home study in my path because He knew you were Justin and Seth's dad. You know, if you want to hear God laugh, tell Him your plan—your plan for much younger children."

I cannot believe how nervous meeting two children can make one grown man. Today is the day. I drive what seems like forever. I arrive at the bowling alley—full of butterflies in my stomach. I walk in and see two boys and the crazy social worker. She really does know what she is talking about. The bowling was a lot of fun and filled up any silent moments during our visit. I was not in-formed prior to our meeting but, I guess there is a secret word for when children have had enough with the time they are spending with a potential family. We must not have had it used. After bowl-ing we all went out to dinner. These boys were amazing boys, but boys too old for my arbitrary age requirement. Already I couldn't imagine a life without them. Now what? The social worker stated that she would be driving the boys back to their foster homes and would call me when she was finished—talk about the longest two hours of my life.

I finally received a call. The social worker asked how I thought the play date went. I could barely put it into words. I explained that Seth was adorable and I was shocked at the fact that Justin, though outside that arbitrary age limit of mine, felt like he was already my son. I quickly asked what the next step was. She explained that she would be talking to the boys. She explained that due to Justin's age, he had the choice to be adopted or not; he actually had to consent to the adoption. Before, I really thought that this was just me making the choices. I never thought a child could veto me. I actually like the idea of a child having some power in their own lives. This is probably the first time in their lives they have had the ability to have any say in how their life will go.

Next there were more phone calls and more play dates. The most exciting news is that both boys have decided that living with me forever is what they want. Justin has made it clear he is not going to call me "Dad" and will not be changing his name. All of this is fine with me. These are things we have time to talk about, and they may never change. I didn't want to adopt so that I can pass on my family name. "Dad" is just a title; being a dad is more than a title.

Prior to having the boys move in and begin our family, there were some details that needed to be put in order. The concern about the possibility of sexually acting out behaviors has to be addressed in our home. The department addresses these types of concerns with a safety plan. This was not in my plans for a family. The social worker explained that the safety plan had to be in place as long as the department was part of our lives, and once the adoption was finalized, the plan would be dismissed. It would be my responsibility as the parent to safeguard both of my children. This is how crazy a safety plan, or at least ours, looks:

- Bedrooms are only for sleeping.
- Justin is not allowed in Seth's room, and vice versa.
- Safety alarms shall be installed on all bedroom doors so as to provide auditory warning of when someone enters a room.
- Family activities such as games shall take place in common areas and shall be utilized to maintain tracking of all children within the home.

Alarms on doors seem a bit extreme, but safety is necessary, and this is only until we finalize the adoption. I installed the alarms, and we completed a family meeting to explain to the boys that bedrooms are off limits except to sleep. We are ready.

The end of the school year was a great time to transition. Summer camps, tutoring, and meeting and visiting new family were all made possible without the distraction of school day to day. The social worker who I used to consider my stalker has now become my dearest friend and someone I will always be grateful to. I cannot think of having a life without my boys. I call, text, and e-mail fairly regularly to provide updates on our boys. Here are a few examples of the messages I've sent her:

- Tutoring is going great; reading has become a preferred activity as opposed to a chore.
- New friends are being made at camp.
- Justin called my dad "Grandpa"!
- Seth called me "Dad" today.
- Justin said it in a whisper, but he said that he loved me today. [I had to call to explain this one.]
- You will not believe what happened today. Seth had a really bad day. He woke up really late, ripped his pants, forgot his lunch, fell on the playground, and went to bed in a completely yucky mood. Justin has followed every safety plan rule up to today without fail. I was tucking Seth in bed when all of a sudden, Justin comes running into Seth's room and jumps on top of him on his bed and kisses him square on the lips. Justin looks down at him and simply asks, "Better?" Seth breaks out in a big smile and says, "Yes. Thank you." I just sat next to Seth's bed in shock. I turned to Justin and asked, "What was that?" He smiled and said, "I know being in Seth's room is against the house rules, but sometimes when

Seth has really bad days, you just have to squish the yuk out of him." All I could think to say was "That's good to know."

Maybe if state agencies were not so quick to think the worst, they also would have known what Justin has always known and what I now know: sometimes Seth just needs the yuk squished out of him. Maybe we all do.

Today was an amazing day. It is National Adoption Day, and we are officially a family. Justin has agreed to change his name as long as he can keep his original last name as his middle name. Seth has been calling me "Dad" on a regular basis, and Justin does the majority of the time. This Thanksgiving, we'll have a lot to be thankful for.

And now it is hard to believe that it has been a full year since we finalized our adoption and became a real family. It has been a very busy year, so I have some catching up to do. The boys have been able to visit with their sisters on a regular basis. Birthdays, holidays, and "just because" visits have become a regular part of our lives. My first name is never used. I am always Dad. Justin has been coming home with only our last name on his school work. He no longer uses his middle name on everything.

Justin has heard our story retold numerous times at this point. I have shared how we became a family to friends and family, and at the agency trainings the boys and I are taking part in. As a family we decided that we have a lot to say about the importance of adopting siblings and older children. Our pictures are even now part of the agency advertisements.

We are enjoying our second Thanksgiving as a real family. We came together with our extended family to celebrate Thanksgiving. As a family we go around the table stating what we are thankful for. Seth, always having food in mind, is thankful for turkey and pie. As we turn the corner of the table, my head is brought up from its bowed position when I hear that Justin is thankful for his family's stalker. I can't hold back my smile and my tears. *Thank you, miss stalker social worker!* ☺

⌖ ⌖

Seth and Justin's father has provided me, **the caseworker**, with numerous updates through the years. Each one has made me cry, all happy tears. The first time Justin called him Dad—tears. The boys choosing to share their story with other possible adoptive families so that other kids like them could someday have a family even though they weren't babies anymore—tears. Justin's graduation from high school with a high GPA—tears. Justin's acceptance into two different universities—many tears. The biggest sobbing was when I was sent a link to Justin's senior class thank-you video to their parents. Justin clearly understands what a forever family is and how his Dad's unconditional love has made a difference in his life.

CHAPTER 6

RONNIE

I am Ronnie, and I should warn you before you start reading, my story may make you sick and mad and maybe even make you cry. I know that in living my life I have been sick and really mad, have cried a lot, and basically seriously screwed up for a long time.

I am the oldest of seven kids—that I know of. I say that because I have been told about new kids my mother has had since I was taken away from her. Now that I am older, I can say that she never should have had one kid, let alone seven, or whatever today's count is.

I was four years old in my first memory of my mother and some of my brothers and sister. Some would say I was too young to actually remember things, but when you experience such traumatic things, you would be surprised what you actually remember. So as I was saying, I was four years old. My baby sister, who hadn't had her first birthday party yet, had been sick for a few days and hadn't stopped crying. I remember all of us going and sitting at the hospital while the doctor looked at Baby. He gave Mom a couple bottles of medicine to make Baby feel better. When we got home Mom gave Baby medicine on a spoon. Baby kept crying. Mom put her on the floor, sat on her, and poured the rest of the bottle of medicine in Baby's mouth. Then Mom went and got a second bottle of medicine and poured that in Baby's mouth too. Baby finally stopped crying but started shaking and flopping on the floor. Mom called someone, and an ambulance came to our house. They took Baby to the hospital. When Mom came back, she didn't bring Baby home. She told us that we were going to go say good-bye to Baby in a couple of days. I remember that a few days later, we went to a cemetery and put Baby in the ground.

The next day a lady from CPS (Child Protective Services) came to talk to us. She asked me a whole bunch of questions and I had to tell her what happened to Baby. I can tell you know I have learned that I actually was watching Baby die. For the record, it is hard to remember watching my mother pour medicine into Baby's mouth and then watching Baby shake and flop on the floor. Knowing now that the minute she stopped shaking she was dead was really hard to live with when I was younger. The CPS lady took me; my twin, Ray; and our other brother and sister to a family to stay while they talked to Mom. We stayed with the family for a few weeks but then went home. Mom explained that the CPS people were wrong. She said that she didn't kill Baby. The doctor gave her the wrong medicine for Baby. It sure looked like she had something to do with Baby dying, seeing as she is the one who gave Baby so much medicine.

My next major memory about Mom's new baby was after my fifth birthday, when she was born. It is sad, but the new baby was only at our house for such a short time; I can't even remember her name anymore. I feel really bad that I can't remember her name, but I remember why she left. New baby came home with Mom from the hospital and cried a lot like Baby did. Mom didn't give her any medicine, though. She did sit her on the couch and turned her face into the back of the cushion. New baby stopped crying and was real still just like Baby. We had the ambulance come to the house again, and we went back to the cemetery. I knew what this meant. New baby had died, and I watched it happen. Mom said that she was gone because she had SIDS. I am much older now and know what SIDS is and that is not what happened to the new baby. She just couldn't breathe with her face in the couch cushions. I did learn that when a baby is said to have SIDS, the rest of us kids don't have to go see a new family while CPS talks to Mom.

Mom and her new boyfriend brought another new baby home. It was my sixth birthday. I remember her name; it was Tina. Tina was gone before Easter. Oh, for the record, my birthday is in January. Mom didn't hurt Tina, but her boyfriend wasn't very nice. She was a baby, and babies cry sometimes. He must not like babies to cry. He didn't give her any medicine or put her face in the couch. All he did was shake her really, really hard. I didn't think that shaking someone could kill them, but as I watched him, I could see around the corner that she stopped moving and looked just like Baby and the new baby did when they were dead.

I really don't think a kid who is only six should see three of his sisters die.

Tina being dead was much different than Baby and the new baby. When a baby like Tina gets shaken up, it breaks things inside of her. Mom's boyfriend went to jail for breaking her. Ray and me and our other brother and sister went to live with different families. I asked the CPS lady why we all couldn't go to the same family. She told me that since Ray and me had one dad and the others had a different dad, there were different families for us. I don't understand, but she is an adult, so she must be right. This time we had to stay with the new family for a very long time. We were there past my seventh birthday.

One day the CPS lady told us we didn't have our mom as our mom anymore and this new family was going to be our mom and dad now. I guess that is fair since we have been here so long and they haven't killed anyone like our mom did.

So Ray and me stayed with this new family until my eighth birthday. I was told I was always bad, and this family sent me to a place that didn't have moms or dads. I had a bedroom with a bunch of other kids. A whole bunch of us bad kids stayed at this place and went to school here too. My mom and dad stopped coming to see me one day. The CPS lady still came to see me and told me my new mom and dad were no longer my mom and dad either. I asked her why, 'cause they didn't kill anyone like my first mom did. I asked her when I was going to see Ray 'cause we are twins and we go everywhere together and do everything together. She told me the other mom and dad wanted to keep Ray, just not me, and I wouldn't be seeing him anymore. I told her I didn't understand. She tried really hard to explain that sometime, even though it is wrong, moms and dads can't handle it when kids are bad. I told her I was having a problem with missing all my sisters. I have really bad dreams about when they died, thoughts about me dying or that I should be dying and a bunch of stuff. The CPS lady talked to one of the staff here about what I had said. All of a sudden I was sleeping in the hall outside the office. I was told that when I wasn't talking about being dead anymore, I could go back to my room. I had to take more medicine and talk to the special doctor a lot more. The special doctor is my therapist. Basically, he is just someone I have to talk to all the time. I get taken to his office a lot more after I said that I should be dead too.

I am not stupid, and I figured out what I have to do to not sleep in the hall, take less medicine, and even get to leave this place and go to a new family with a mom and dad. I stopped talking about my sisters who are dead; Ray, who I never see anymore; my first mom; and even my second mom and dad. *Tada, magic.* I get to move out.

My new family lives in a really big house that is out in the country, is super clean, and has pretty stuff everywhere. I like this house, and I like getting to go to church with them. They have a place at church with lots of kids as old as me. We do all sorts of cool things.

I like being here right now and am trying really hard to be good and not think about my dead sisters or Ray. I haven't thought about my other brother and sister for a long time 'cause I was already told they have a different family 'cause we had different dads. I figured a long time ago that they are not my brother and sister anyway.

The harder I try not to think of the sisters and Ray, the harder it gets. I asked my CPS lady once if I could see Ray or go to the cemetery to see my sisters, and she said she would see. That was a while ago, and nothing has happened. I got a new CPS lady and asked her too. She claimed that she didn't know where they were. *Really, how is that possible?* I thought. I asked her again, and she just said no. That is not fair. I thought for a long time. I have been really good and haven't been getting into any trouble, and I still haven't been able to see Ray anyway. Maybe if I misbehave, I could go see him or at least my sisters. So here goes.

Today when I woke up, all I could think about was seeing my brother. He is my brother. He is my twin. I know that the worse I behave, the better my chances are to see him or at least be taken to the cemetery to say hi to my sisters even though they can't say anything to me. I had to go number one and two when I woke up, so I just lay in the bed and went. It was really gross, but boy, was it bad. When the mom of the house came in, she was so upset. She sent the dad into take care of me. He got me out of bed and helped remove the sheets from the bed and into the washer. He told me to go take a shower. Really, the bed should have been bad enough. I stood in the shower but didn't use any soap and didn't stand under the water. I waited long enough to make it seem like I had washed. I got out and took a towel and rubbed the poop all over me and then the rest of the bathroom. This is so gross, I hope this works. When I came out of the bathroom, the dad was not happy with me and sent me back into the bathroom and told me to use soap. Nope, he couldn't make me. Since he is a guy too, it was OK for him to stand in the bathroom while I was made to wash. I couldn't figure out how else to get around it so I used the soap and got real clean. I guess even though I had already been bad, I had to get clean in order to go and see Ray. I didn't want him to think I was one of those kids that poops his pants. I got dressed and immediately asked when we were going to see Ray. I was told that type of behavior was not going to get me to see Ray, just the therapist. Off we went, and I had to sit and talk to him about my morning. I just told him that I was going to go see my brother finally and was going to keep getting more and more bad to make sure that it happened. He tried to explain that the type of behavior I was doing was not going to help in me seeing Ray. He tried to explain that Ray had been adopted by the second mom and dad, and they would not allow me to see him. It had nothing to do with how good or bad I was. I didn't believe him.

The days came and went. I did so many bad things and nothing seemed to work. I broke the pretty things in the house, pooped in my bed, started hitting the mom, and basically didn't listen to anything I was told to do. I can be so much worse than any adult can imagine. It didn't work. I didn't get to see Ray or my sisters but did end up going back to the place with all the kids and staff and school at the same place. I had to take lots of medicine, which just made me want to do nothing. I had to talk to the therapist all the time. He tried to help me understand why I can't see Ray or my sisters and how important it was for me to behave so I could find a forever family of my own. I am trying to understand, but it really doesn't make sense.

I got a new CPS worker again. It is so cool; her son and me have the same birthday. She is really nice. I didn't know that CPS ladies have kids of their own. She tried to help me understand why I might actually like to have my own family. When I was really good, she even took me to have a milk shake. I am only allowed to go out in town when I have green cards on the board. I like going out in town with my CPS lady and try to have lots of green cards now. She came to see me today. I have had all green cards for a long time. We went to get an ice cream today. When we were out, we talked about me getting out of the facility and going to a new home. I asked if this was going to be forever. She said she wouldn't promise that because part of the decision was up to me, and the other part was up to the family once I had been there a little while.

Today was the day that I got to go to my new home. It was hard saying good-bye to all the friends I had made at the facility and all the staff that took care of me. I even had to say good-bye to my therapist. He said he was so proud of me and all the progress I have made. I am proud of me too. I am very excited about meeting my new family. He reminded me that being bad does not equal seeing my brother or sisters. He reminded me that not being able to see my brother was the fault of his mom and dad, and not Ray's or my fault. I told him I remembered that I was getting older, and when we are adults we can make our own decisions and might be able to see each other then. I am having my fourteenth birthday after Christmas is over. It has been seven years since I have seen Ray, and my sisters have been gone for so long. I only have four years before Ray and me are eighteen, and then I can see him for sure. I promised my therapist I was going to make good decisions from now on.

My new family lives in a big town with lots of neighbors with kids and lots of kids in the house. We are always busy doing things that are lots of fun. We have to do our schoolwork in order to go to the pool or out to eat. I am really trying to be good like I told my therapist I would. It is so hard. I have been bad for so long that deep inside I still think I might be able to see Ray if I am bad. I tried it a couple times. My new mom and dad were not like the others. They seemed to know what I was doing. They told me that acting like that wasn't going to get me anywhere. How did they know what I was up too? They told me this wasn't their first rodeo. The look on my face must have been one of "*What?*" They explained they have had lots of kids live with them, and they all would try to do bad stuff to get what they wanted. They told me that doesn't work in their house. I did try a few more times, and it still didn't work.

Today when I woke up, I decided that all my efforts weren't going to work, so I asked my mom what would work so that I could see my brother or sisters. She explained the exact same thing that my therapist had. It was not up to her, my CPS lady, or even the courts to allow me to see Ray. She said that she knew it wasn't fair, but his new parents had adopted him, and it was totally up to them. She did say that if she can find out where my sisters are at, she would fight to get permission to go see them. I have never had anyone say I might actually get to go. Wow, she must really love me like she keeps saying she does. My CPS lady came to see us today also. My mom asked where my sisters were buried. She told Mom but stated it may not be a good idea to go to the cemetery. Mom said that she would talk to my therapist first and let me talk to him before we went. I was so excited that I wanted to go to the therapist today. This was not the day for seeing him, but at least I knew there was a really good chance I could see them if he said it was OK.

It seems like it has been forever, but today I got to go tell my therapist how much I wanted to see my sisters. We talked for a long time, and he finally said he would talk to my mom about going sometime soon. I could hardly stand it. I ran into the waiting room and told my mom that I could go. I was jumping up and down and asked if we were going right now. She made me take a deep breath (she has me do that a lot) and sit down while she went and talked to the therapist. I knew what he was going to tell her 'cause he told me what he was going to say. He told her it had been many years and I was very young when my sisters had died. I had watched the painful experiences of their deaths, and saying a real good-bye was very important and part of what I needed to help me heal. I felt like telling everyone who had ever been in my life that I was right all along. This is important and what I needed. The therapist said so, *yes!*

Today is the day. I am so excited and so scared. I don't know what to expect. I have wanted this for so long, but right now I am not sure that I really want this. *YES, I do*, I think again. If I don't go today, I may never be given another chance. I got dressed in my best pants and shirt, almost like I was going to church. I know they can't see me, but I felt like they would like it if I looked really nice. I couldn't even eat breakfast, I was so nervous. Mom said we would get something if I wanted after we had visited my sisters. We drove forever. I didn't think we would ever get there. I didn't know how many people actually go to the cemetery. I don't remember seeing so many rocks with peoples' names on them when we were here before. I was only six, I think, when Tina died, so it would be easy to forget. Mom told me that the rocks with all the names on them are called tombstones. Before we got to Baby's, the new baby's (whose name I can't remember), and Tina's tombstones, Mom explained there are a bunch of sizes and some just sit on the ground flat. She pointed to one on the ground and explained that these people are just as important and special to their families as my sisters are to me. It is just that some families like little stones and some like the really big ones, kind of like cars. I know that what she was saying is that some people have money to buy big tombstones and some don't. I know my first mom didn't have a lot of money, so my sisters weren't going to have very big stones.

We finally made it to the place where the man in the office said my sisters would be. They were all next to each other. For some reason I felt good to know that they were next to each other all this time. They didn't have any flowers on their tombstones like a lot of the other people, but that was OK 'cause Mom and me brought them daisies. I now know all my sisters names 'cause they are marked into their tombstones. I had baby sisters who were as follows:

- Reannah Kim (Baby): Born February 14 and died January 10; not even a year old. I stood there for the longest time. She died on my birthday, and I didn't even remember that.
- Rebekkeah Kaylyn (new baby): Born January 31 and died March 31; she was only two months old, no wonder I couldn't remember her name. She was born right after Baby died and didn't even see her birthday.
- Tinnetta Kirlin (Tina): Born January 10 and died March 31. Unbelievable. She was born on my birthday and died on the same day as Rebekkeah.

It felt like I stood there forever. I gave each of my sisters some daisies and imagined that they were smiling. Mom reminded me that though they were not on this earth very long, they had known that I loved them, and they could feel my love today since I brought them flowers and had fought so hard to see them. I must have thanked my Mom a thousand times for letting me see my sisters. She gave me a really big hug. We sat on the ground and she let me read them the book that I had brought with me. It was a baby story, *Love You Forever* by Robert Munsch, that I thought I had when I was little, but the truth is, I have no idea. Maybe it was just a book that I had hoped I had when I was little. It was a very happy story and reminded the babies how much they were loved. I read the book a couple of times, actually once to each of my sisters, and then we put the book on Baby's tombstone since she was the oldest of them. Mom asked if I was ready to go. I paused for a minute and asked if we would ever be able to come back. I told her that it made me feel so much better to know that someone was here to read to them and bring them flowers. I told her they were too young to be forgotten.

We wrote down their birthdays, and Mom said we would try really hard to come and visit on their birthdays at least. I couldn't thank her enough. I knew that coming more often would be really hard since it seemed like we drove forever to get here. Even if we never get to go back, I learned a lot about my sisters and know I will always love them even if I only had them in my life for such a short time. I know they deserved to be loved and never deserved to die. I also learned how much my mom loves me. She took an entire day away from everyone else to let me see them, take them flowers, and read them a story that I think was my favorite. She sat with me for a very long time and made me feel like I was the most important person in the world. I don't think I ever said thank you or told her how much it meant to me, but if she ever reads this: Thank you, Mom.

⇒⊱ ⊰⇐

We are Bob and Samantha (Sam). Ronnie came to us after his many foster home placements and countless visits to inpatient treatment. He is not the first child we have had placed with us. We have been foster parents for many years and have always had placement of difficult children. All the children we have had in our home have had extreme behaviors. We have specialized training in order to work with these very special children who seem to be difficult to place in regular foster homes. We consider ourselves to be strictly foster parents and have never considered adopting. There are some homes identified as foster/adoptive homes, which are usually families that really want to adopt but have been told it is easier to have a child placed with them as a foster care placement first. Once again, this is not us. There are many children in the foster care system and not nearly enough foster homes. When we originally discussed becoming foster parents, we decided that foster care was all we wanted to do. It has been our experience that placing a child who is free for adoption in our care comes with questions of if we are interested in adopting. We have always made it clear to the caseworker and our case manager that this was not going to be our intention. We would assist in preparing the child for adoption and be a strong resource for transitioning him or her into his or her adoptive family home. Transitioning a child into his or her adoptive home can be quite a bit of work. It is not just food, clothing and shelter. It is extreme counseling, additional visits with potential adoptive families once they are identified, and transporting the child for photos or video shoots or any other activity that can assist in recruiting an adoptive family.

In Ronnie's case there were even more activities to help in preparing him for adoption. Ronnie came to us with more baggage than most other children who have been placed in our home. We have been used to children suffering from physical, emotional, and even sexual abuse in their families of origin as well as neglect. Ronnie's memories of siblings he had lost and adoptive families that had given up on him made the idea of adoption difficult to embrace. Why should he want to be adopted again when one family had already shown him that a "forever family" means nothing? All he had known in his life was loss: loss of siblings who had not just died but died violently in front of him; loss of biological parents; loss of adoptive parents who didn't want him; and loss of his brother, who his adoptive parents did want. Where do we start?

Like the song "Do-Re-Mi" from *The Sound of Music* says, we started at the very beginning, as it is a very good place to start. Ronnie's trouble starts with the numerous losses of his sisters who had died. When he asked to visit their graves, we immediately started the fight with the caseworker. We were already committed to the transportation to numerous appointments with doctors, counselors, and adoption activities, but none of that would matter if we didn't visit the cemetery first. The only way to help Ronnie was to address the first traumas of his life.

We never thought so many people would be against taking steps to help a child heal. Even though his caseworker was in agreement with us, we had to battle with the supervisor, the upper management, and even the court. After months of therapy visits, which resulted in documentation from the therapist that it was in fact in Ronnie's best interest to address his early childhood trauma, the approvals were granted. We were off to visit the cemetery where his sisters were buried. We ensured that he would have a therapy appointment later in the day of the scheduled cemetery visit. Saying good-bye to his sisters and having some closure was not enough. He would have to process a whole bunch of feelings that came with the visit. We knew he would be open to talking to us, as he had been up to this point, but sometimes it is helpful to have a professional with whom Ronnie has developed a strong relationship.

You have never seen such a nervous yet excited child as Ronnie was when he woke up the morning of the visit to his sisters. It was a long drive, which meant there was going to be a lot of time going and coming home to talk or else have a large gap of silence. I have always had a compact DVD player in our car for long trips, so I made sure that Ronnie picked out a few of his favorite movies. I explained to him that the movies would be in the car if he wanted to watch them, but I would be in the car also and would love to talk at any time he wanted. As Ronnie was known for, I got a simple "'K" response. We got on the road.

There was initially a lot of chatter on the trip to the cemetery. Ronnie had a lot of questions. How far is it, did we bring snacks, are we allowed to stop for the bathroom, how much time do we get to visit, and what time is his therapy appointment? The questions were answered as they were asked: two hours, no snacks but we could stop for some if he was hungry, we will stop for bathroom breaks if needed, and we would stay as long as he wanted to visit. I explained that we could always reschedule the therapy appointment if we didn't make it back in time. I further explained that his time with his sisters was the most important thing right now. When we pulled into the town, we stopped for a bathroom trip before going to visit his sisters. I could see how nervous and scared Ronnie seemed. He even commented that he felt like he was "facing his demons." I am sure that this is a term that he has heard too often in therapy or from some doctors who were trying to help him process his past. Either way, it was clear that this was how he truly felt. I tried to reassure him that there were no demons here, just his sisters' graves, and they were in an amazing place looking down on him and would be very excited that he had fought so hard to come see them. Ronnie thanked me for being the one to come with him. He stated that no matter what, he knew it was going to be OK 'cause his mom was with him. I gave him a big hug and loaded us back into the car. We arrived at the cemetery, and he sat still for what seemed like forever. Ronnie finally reached for his door but first picked up the books he had brought with him. We walked around and finally found the tiny name plates that marked his sisters' graves. He stated that they were so tiny and asked why they didn't get the really big stones like other people. I explained that the big ones are bought by people with a lot of money and are like people who drive big fancy cars. Ronnie laughed and stated, "That's stupid, they are dead and can't even see the fancy stones."

Ronnie and I spread a blanket on the ground and got comfy. He introduced me to each of his sisters and retold their stories as he remembered them. I asked him to tell me something special that he remembered about each of them. He shared smiles, curls, and eye and hair color, and then, with a frown, he stated that he couldn't remember anything more. I reassured him that was OK because he remembered what was most important; he remembered that he loved them. He remembered to fight hard enough to be able to come visit them. Ronnie read them the books he had brought and gave them each flowers and a teddy bear. After sitting quiet for a while, he asked if he could leave the books with them in case someone else wanted to read to them. I stated that was a great idea. He said he was ready to go but would rather go home if that was OK. He stated that he would talk to his therapist another day about how he was feeling but that today was about his sisters and not him. What a mature young man I have.

The ride home was very quiet, and when I looked into the rear-view mirror, I realized he had fallen asleep. I am sure that it had been a very long, exhausting day. I am truly blessed to have been able to share this with Ronnie.

It has been several months since our trip to see Ronnie's sisters. He has been talking to his therapist about it and processing a lot of emotions. As expected, with the emotions came new behaviors, which led to a trip to the inpatient unit to stabilize his mental health and reevaluate medications. We knew this was not going to be a miracle cure, and by no means was it going to make things easier. We did know that it was exactly what Ronnie needed, and in the long run it was our prayer that it would create some healing.

Now, a year after the visit with his sisters, Ronnie asked if he could stay with us forever. He shared that he has never had anyone love him for so long; put up with so much and not throw him away. I pulled my baby boy into the biggest bear hug and told him that I couldn't imagine a life without him. That night when my husband got home, I told him that we would be calling the case-worker to start the adoption process. He reminded me that we had agreed that we do not adopt, we foster. I asked him what his life would look like without Ronnie in it. He looked at me and said he couldn't imagine it, nor did he want to. "Decision made; we are adopting our son."

Ronnie turned nineteen this past January. The day was a little delayed due to all the changes in foster homes and treatment centers, but it had come: Ronnie graduated from high school this June. I of course cried; this is my happy response to life. Would he have made it to graduation without us? *Probably.* Would he have worked through so many demons that haunted his dreams and daily life? *Maybe.* Would our lives been so complete, so full of love and so many blessings, had we not adopted Ronnie? *Without a doubt, NO, NO, NO.*

CHAPTER 7
CASEY

I am Casey, and I have been in foster care for seven years. I didn't start in foster care, but it seems like I did. The years prior to care are so long ago that they start to get blurry sometimes. Maybe they really aren't that blurry, but it's more I'm just trying to block them out for good. The small problem with blocking them out all together is that then I would lose all my siblings who I already miss desperately. For the longest time, my memories of them was all I had. Maybe I should try to go back a few years. I should apologize if my thoughts travel around in time, but that is kind of how my memories are anyway. I can't really tell you stuff in order when I can't remember the order of myself. You will just have to keep up, stay confused, or give up. Please don't give up; people do that way too often.

I am the youngest of eight children. With all the other kids I have been in care with, I have determined that there are a lot of really big families—well, at least in foster care. This is really sad because every kid I have come across isn't in the same foster home with their siblings, and most can't remember the last time they had all their brothers and sisters in the same place. I have my oldest sister, Martha, in Montana. She is an adult and got as far from this place as she could. I would like that too. Most days I think she had the right idea: run from here and leave all the ugly stuff behind. She seems really happy and has kids of her own now. I haven't seen her in what seems like forever, but we send letters and have talked on the phone. I keep asking to go on vacation to see her, but when you are a kid in foster care, there are all these rules. Martha has to have a background check, and so does everyone in her house. No one seems to be able to figure out how to do this. The other option is to have someone here have a background check done and then take me to see my sister. See, this way the state can say that I was with a responsible adult. Whatever, it never seems to happen. I have been promised it so many times, but it never fails—some supervisor, director, or something stops it.

I have another sister, Pam, who is just two years older than me, and we live in the same town. It should be easy to set up visits, right? Well, we actually were placed together for a while, but to be honest, I was pretty screwed up and got in a lot of trouble. I didn't last in that foster home very long, but my sister stayed. I am not sure how, but I have learned that there are different ways for kids to stay in one home. You can go home with your parents, but I haven't seen this happen. You can be adopted by a new family, which is what I want more than anything. Then there is this legal thing where someone can take permanent responsibility for you but doesn't have to adopt you. I still don't see the purpose of this. You still have to go to court even though it is only once a year, still have a social worker, and still need everyone and God's permission to do anything. I want my own family with no court, social workers, etc. I want to be able to just ask my mom and dad for permission like my friends do.

Anyway, Pam is with a family who didn't adopt her, but they have that permanent thing. I thought that if she still had court and a part-time social worker, then they would be able to make decisions about what she can and can't do like visiting me. Well, I learned that this is not the case at all. I have been told that Pam's foster parents who got this court-ordered nonadoption thing can say who she can and cannot see. You guessed it; I am not on her visitors list. She isn't even going to the same school anymore. I am not sure where she is going, but it is probably so we can't run into each other. I would love to take the brothers and sisters of some of these adults away and see how they feel. I don't care if you like me or not. Sibs are important, and we should be allowed to see each other.

One of the kids who lived in the same foster home got to go to this camp this year. It is called Camp To Belong (www.campto-belong.org) and is where sibs can get together for a whole week in the summer. I asked if I could do this with Pam, but, of course, the adults of my siblings had to be willing to send them to the same camp. You guessed it; that never happened.

I had other brothers and sisters who were taken from my mother long before me. The difference was they had different fathers than my other two sisters. They all got to go live with their dads, who turned out to actually be good guys and loved their children. I am not sure how it worked out, but my mother hooked up with the same man for Martha, Pam, and me. The other five had two different dads. Somehow my dad was a deadbeat, but their dads were great. It doesn't really matter how all the men came and went in my mother's life. What matters is that Pam, Martha, and me ended up with no backup plan like a dad, so foster care was the only option for us. Luckily for Martha, she turned eighteen before our mother became a useless parent.

I guess I haven't shared that part, have I. I am trying to figure out if there was ever a good time in our family. Our mother had to have had good times since she had five kids who had great dads. I don't remember that. I remember Martha taking care of me and Pammy. Martha would fix whatever food was in the house or steal what she could to make sure we ate. Martha would make sure we got on the bus. She would sign all the school papers to make sure that we got free lunch and school breakfast. Now that I think about it, I should have been calling Martha "Mom." The woman who gave birth to us was anything but a mother. She was a slut, crack whore, and angry bitch. Yeah, I have no positive memories of her. Sometimes the bad stuff just casts such a big shadow you can't even see the good stuff anymore.

I have tried to sit here quiet to see if a happy time actually comes to mind. I came up with a birthday with all my brothers and sisters and my own dad. I remember him as a great guy. I had presents and a cake. I had to come up with all sorts of memories for when I have been in therapy. The helpful thing is that my therapist always has had the file with the facts, so she has been able to help me piece together memories. I guess it is supposed to help with healing. I don't know that I believe that. She helped me remember when everything fell apart in our world. My dad was not a deadbeat who wasn't willing to care for us. He was a sick man who ate his gun. I must admit, there is no kid who needs to remember that. I don't need healing or closure from something I didn't remember in the first place. Now I do remember, but how do you get past the vision of your dad like that? Someday someone will have to explain that to me.

Sorry, but that is enough of that. I would rather talk about how far I have come, how I turned a corner, and how I found home. Like I said in the beginning, I have been in care for five years. I jumped around to a lot of foster homes and new schools, with lots of lost friends, and I finally landed in a home that works, though it has screwed-up teenage girls. I finally landed where I needed to be since I also feel like a screwed-up teenager most of the time. The parents were a strong support to me. I stayed in therapy, worked hard in school, and finally stopped getting into trouble. It is amazing, when you have a family that doesn't give up on you, how much easier it is not to give up on yourself. With the Clarks' help, I was on less medication to stabilize my behaviors and emotions and only had to go to therapy twice a month. My grades in school were amazing. If there weren't report cards as proof, no one would have believed I was in honors classes and on the A/B honor roll. How is this possible? Well, the Clarks told me and my social worker they wanted to adopt me. If you recall, this is what I have wanted. I have wanted a real family of my own. I know they have never adopted before, so this would be a first for them. It really makes me feel even more important and loved to think that there has never been any other kids they loved as much as they love me.

So we had this meeting, and my foster parents told everyone they wanted to adopt me, and this made it official. It was explained they would have to have an adoptive home study even though they were already foster parents. They were told that this was policy and due to federal law (the Adam Walsh Act). They would have to have new fingerprint checks. Another social worker who only does home studies came to the meeting and gave the Clarks a bunch of paperwork. I was so excited I could hardly stand it. The other social worker and my worker explained that the adoption could be completed in as little as three to six months if they got the home study papers back quickly.

Three to six months turned out to be BS. My social worker explained that the Clarks hadn't turned in the papers yet. When she tried to talk to them, there was always a reason why things weren't moving faster. A bunch of times they blamed me, saying that I was acting like I didn't want to be adopted and that I needed to go to more therapy, be back on medication, etc. My school grades are still amazing. I volunteer with Habitat for Humanity and am in clubs at school. Most parents would love a kid like me. I am so confused. It has been over a year since the Clarks said they wanted to adopt me. Nothing has happened. I am sixteen already.

I got a new social worker, and she decided we needed to have another meeting to clarify what the Clarks were going to do. Since

I still wanted to be adopted, she said that is what she is going to work at making happen. Well, the meeting took place but was pretty depressing. The Clarks changed their minds and made me feel like it was all my fault. It must be so easy to blame the screwed-up foster kid for everything. I can't handle even being in the same house with any of them anymore. How do you tell a kid that you will love them forever but aren't willing to give them the one thing that would make them happiest? I wasn't asking for a car like most sixteen-year-olds or a spring break trip to the tropics. I want a family of my own.

I saw my social worker a few weeks later. I was supposed to hang out with my bestest friend, so I asked if she could come along. She explained there was some stuff that she wanted to talk to me about, and as long as I didn't mind talking in front of her, it was fine. My social worker took us out for coffee so we could talk away from the foster home and not have to worry about people listening in.

My social worker skipped her generic questions this visit: no "How is school?" "What is for dinner?" etc. We had already talked about a lot of that on the phone when we were setting up the visit.

She jumped right in and asked, "What do you want?"

I was very clear about the question and came back with a prompt response, "I want to be adopted!"

She asked about looking for a family in a different town or even state. I explained how important it was to finish school where I was. I was a junior and was so active at my school. It wasn't right that I should have to leave. She explained she would keep looking, but she hadn't found any families in this area who were interested in adopting a sixteen-year-old.

Then she asked a question that I didn't even know was an option. "Casey, do you have any friends' parents or teachers that you are close to who would consider adopting you?"

My besty chimed in without even talking to me first. She said, "Casey is already my sister and spends a lot of time at my house. She calls my mom and dad 'Mom and Dad.' Can they adopt her and then we could be real sisters?"

I looked across at my social worker and said, "*Well?*"

She asked to have my besty's parents call her and gave me her personal cell phone so that we didn't have to wait till morning. I was shocked. This may be too good to be true. I asked my social worker to please not say anything to the foster parents because it was just going to make things much more stressful than they already were at the foster home. She agreed.

I don't really know all the conversations between the adults, so here is my social worker to fill in the gaps.

⇥ ⇤

As I have been introduced, **I am the social worker**. I did talk to Casey and her best friend, Kelsey, about the idea of adoption. Kelsey said that she would give her parents my number to call immediately. I was not going to hold my breath. I have known kids, including my own, to make promises for their parents when the parent has no idea of what is going on and no interest. Adopting a child, especially one who is sixteen and out of foster care, is a huge undertaking to ask of anyone.

I didn't even make it to my front porch when my phone rang. It was Kelsey's mom. She introduced herself and stated that she had some questions about adoption of Casey. She stated that before she went in to her laundry list of questions, I should know that Casey was already their daughter. She explained that she is over as often as she is permitted by the foster parents and she and Kelsey are a positive influence on each other, including doing homework together. She stated she and her husband want nothing more than to make her an official part of their family, but needed to know what this entailed. I took a deep breath before I started. I know that families come together in different ways and can be formed through many avenues, including friends' families, teachers, church members, and so on, but I personally had never experienced this route. It was amazing to know that a family could love so much that they were willing to jump right in. Here we go.

I explained the home study process; fingerprints; adoption support; the lifetime commitment, not just until Casey turned eighteen; court processes and supervision of Casey; and her placement with their family up until the adoption was finalized. I explained that the court process had many different levels. Kelsey's parents, Mr. and Mrs. Thomas, would be required to attend court in order for the court and other parties to know what their intentions were. It was explained that since Casey had been in her foster home for more than a year, the department administration would have to give permission to move her first. Mrs. Thomas was very quiet on the other end of the phone. I was fearful she had been scared off by the overwhelming list of bureaucratic hoops that would need to be jumped through. After a very long silence, Mrs. Thomas stated that she and her husband would do what needed to be done because they loved Casey that much. She asked if I would mind going over the laundry list one more time. I offered to come by at a time that was convenient to both her and her husband to discuss the details so that I could answer all of their questions. Mrs. Thomas was very apologetic and stated this probably wouldn't be possible since their schedules were so crazy; they both wouldn't be available during office hours. I had to laugh. Without hesitation I informed her that her schedule was different: Eight to five means nothing when it comes to the life of a child. We agreed on an 8:00 p.m. visit to their home. Visiting the family home was actually an initial requirement, so taking care of it early on was a double bonus.

—+ +—

Mrs. Thomas here, speaking for Mr. Thomas too, though we would like to be known as Jill and Kyle. We each have been married before, and our family is very blended. We are a "his, mine, and ours" family, though we have never seen it that way. All of our girls act as if they were born as what the world would consider true siblings. There may not be the same blood running through all of their veins, but the blood is not what is seen anyway. What makes up a family is the day-to-day joys and trials and how we support each other through it all. We have never questioned our commitment to each of our children. When we got married, "his and mine" became "ours." Now we are looking at a girl who has been ours since our daughter brought her home. Many of our children's friends have been in our home, so we can't even explain why Casey felt like "our" daughter from day one. She just fit in like one of the sisters. How were we to know that God already knew she was ours? It just took us a while to find each other.

The social worker arrived at our home at 8:00 p.m. on a Friday night. We were still in shock that a state worker would go out of her way to help a child who most would just call "a job." She obviously sees her work as more than a paycheck. I think we thanked her a thousand times and apologized for the inconvenience a thousand more. She was so warm and continued to tell us, "*Stop*. I wouldn't be anywhere else."

We learned that the department makes every effort not to move kids from one foster home to another when a child has been in a home for more than a year. Although this is not always possible, administrative approval must be received in order to move a child, or the move must be court-ordered. The social worker explained that Casey has a lot of people in her life looking out for her best interest. A meeting would be held to discuss the possibility of our family being Casey's adoptive family. We learned that we would meet Casey's attorney and her guardian ad litem (GAL), and we learned what the difference was between the two. An attorney of a child in foster care argues in court for what the child wants even if this isn't the best thing for the child. The GAL fights for what is in the child's best interest. We learned that sometimes this is the same thing and sometime it isn't. We have never been a part of this "adoption world," and it was all very new to us. It is a lot of information to take in. The social worker was very patient and explained terms and people's roles in Casey's life until we assured her we felt comfortable with all the information.

So the bottom line is that everything has to take place in a specific order. The social worker seemed to have this down to a science. So here we go with all the steps. You may want to prepare yourself as we had to, because this is not a quick and simple process.

1. The social worker will schedule the team meeting.
2. The social worker will make a referral for an adoption home study.
3. The social worker will file court document to notify the court about the new family that is interested in adopting Casey.
4. The social worker will document today's home visit as the first step in the home study.
5. The home study social worker will schedule a meeting with us, for which we may have to rearrange our schedule.
6. We will fill out all the home study paperwork.

7. We will complete our fingerprint checks.
8. We will have up to three interviews with the home study social worker.
9. Once permission for administration approval and completed home study are ordered by the court, we will move Casey into our home.
10. We will then allow Casey's social worker access to our home for supervision at least once a month.
11. We will complete adoption support paperwork.
12. We will retain an attorney.
13. We will agree on a day to finalize the adoption.
14. We may need to attend family therapy if any issues are identified after Casey moves in and prior to the finalization of the adoption.

Well, that was the initial list. We experienced some unexpected things along the way, but there wasn't anything that would come between our daughter and us. First, we had to bring her home. We had planned this for a month or so ahead because of the steps with the meetings and administration approval. We forgot about all the people in Casey's life. Her GAL had talked to Casey and us and knew she wanted and needed to be with us as soon as possible. She scheduled a court hearing ASAP. The court ordered her to be placed with us immediately. Kyle went with Casey and the social worker to the foster home, packed her up, and moved her in all in one day, only two weeks after we had reviewed all the steps. Here we thought this was going to drag on forever, and now our baby girl was home. We could only hope that the rest of the list moved along as fast.

We had the first meeting of many with the home study worker and got our fingerprints run immediately. We provided the worker with our pets' immunization records, insurance documentation, and our medical physicals, and we obtained new smoke detectors and bought a fire extinguisher. Our home study should be good to go.

OK, our to-do list was moving right along. Casey was with us, which meant that the social worker visited frequently, which turned out to be a very good thing. Having a new baby makes for a lot of changes in a family. The fact that our new baby was sixteen brought its own changes to our home. We weren't getting up for 2:00 a.m. feedings, but we were dealing with teenage sibling arguments, PMS times four (since we had girls), and quadruple the amount of school activities and homework. There were a few of those sibling fights and PMS days that I would have eagerly traded for a 2:00 a.m. feeding.

Our new daughter didn't come home in a newborn outfit, and we wouldn't have had it any other way. I am sure when our first three daughters entered our home, they were not nearly as nervous as our Casey. Of course, they were newborn babies and have no memory of their welcome home.

Casey celebrated her seventeenth birthday today. We celebrated our new daughter by making it legal that she was ours. There weren't any blankets, bonnets, or booties, but there were bouquets of roses, balloons, and our new baby's teddy bear. It was the cutest thing in the world to see the court give our daughter a teddy bear as a gift to celebrate her adoption.

Now it has been two years since our baby girl officially became ours. We have had our ups and downs. There have been days when hurtful words have been said, like "I would have been better to have stayed in foster care"; "You don't really love me, you just felt sorry for me"; and "You should just send me back then you will all be happy." Despite these negative moments, there have been far more days when love has stood fast in all our hearts. These days have included statements like "I can't imagine life without you"; "I never knew that anyone was capable of loving me so much"; "I can't believe that you love me so much that you put up with all the hurtful things I say"; and "I love you, Mom and Dad." The interesting thing is that a little twist in Casey's wording has come out of the mouths of our birth children: "You don't love her, you just felt sorry for her"; "Can we send her back?"; "I would rather be in foster care"; and "My life would have been better in some other family." It will never cease to amaze me that at the end of the day, every one of our children would give her life for the others, take on the world to protect each other, and forget how to breathe if all of her sisters weren't part of our lives. Every family goes through struggles. Our struggles may look a little different, but we still must struggle through them nonetheless. From day one, we all agreed there would be hard days, so we agreed to have a plan for those days. We signed a contract with each other that not one of us would let the others end a day without reminding each other that we love everyone in our family unconditionally. Not one of us started our lives in this family. We have collected each other through the years, and each one for different reasons.

Casey started college this year. She graduated high school with high honors. She was accepted into the college of her choice, and not the community college that so many foster children default to. One small problem with this is that she now lives in the dorms. Casey calls home regularly to check on her baby sister and to talk to her Mom and Dad. (We never get tired of hearing her call us that.) We received a very odd item in the mail not too long ago. As many people will agree, the mail these days is mostly advertisements and bills; personal correspondence only comes in a text or e-mail, or through Facebook. To receive a letter, handwritten and postmarked from the area of our daughter's college, sent me into instant shock. Our Casey had stopped her day to write an actual letter. I sat in shock as I read—expecting the worst. I was pleasantly surprised that the words I was reading were those of gratitude, love, and love. Yes, that word was typed twice on purpose.

I will stop here with our story to say a special thank you for an unusual social worker who was able to think outside the box, consider an unusual family, and focus only on the love of a child who many would have given up on. Finally, I will encourage any social worker, caseworker, therapist, or whoever works with these very special children by saying, "Don't give up on them *ever.*" They deserve love, and as long as the adults in their lives don't give up, they will find it.

Casey has completed her bachelor's degree in premed and will be starting medical school this coming year. Her parents are so proud of their daughter and brag about her to anyone who will listen.

CHAPTER 8
SAVANNAH

I am Phyllis,. When we were asked to participate in this book and tell our daughter's story, our first response was "No, thank you." Our caseworker was very polite and didn't pressure us to reconsider. She thanked us again, as she had done twelve years ago when we adopted our Savannah. But the night after we said no to telling our story, my husband and I were talking about the start of our family and how little we knew at the time. We talked about how far we had come. We talked about how great it would have been if someone had told us his or her story before we jumped in with both feet. We decided there really wouldn't have been a book to change how we felt about our baby girl, but it might help someone else. Needless to say, we changed our minds and called the caseworker to tell our story. We discussed the purpose for the book, how she would like to tell our story, and the questions began.

Paul and I have been married for 20 years. The first six years of our marriage, we tried everything to have a baby. We never realized how much work, time, energy, and money could go into trying to get pregnant. We both grew up in families with a lot of children, and no one else had these issues. There was obviously something wrong with us. Doctors did all the tests on us and then provided

111

us with a diagnosis as well as a multitude of options for having a baby of our very own. But after five years of being poked, prodded, and treated like test animals, we decided that we were not going to have a baby. We were done trying.

Shortly after throwing in the towel on having a baby of our very own, some friends asked if we had considered adopting. It had never really crossed our minds, as we were too busy being some doctor's science project. We began the research. There are all sorts of adoptions. We could adopt from a foreign country. We could adopt from an agency that works with an unwed mother looking to give her child up for adoption. Or, finally, we could choose the same route as our friend, who was using the foster care system, which provides adoption of a child who has been removed from his or her biological parents because of abuse or neglect. So many choices made for a long discussion and even more soul searching, so we went with a process of research and elimination.

First, foreign adoptions are a long process and can be very costly. This felt like we were buying a baby, which just felt wrong to us. There are so many children within the United States who need a family; why would we want to go searching abroad? We want to make it clear that there is nothing wrong with foreign adoptions; this option just wasn't right for us.

The next option we looked at was adopting, through a local adoption agency, a child of an unwed mother. We talked to several agencies. Each explained the process and the fact that it could take a long time. In this type of adoption, the biological parents could choose the adoptive parents for their child. Wow, the biological parents could *go shopping* for the perfect family for their child! One agency explained that it also works with the state in adopting children in foster care. We thought this could also be an option for us.

Last came the option of adopting a child from foster care. We went on a few websites that have children who are identified as "legally free." We learned quickly that this meant the biological parents no longer had rights to their children; therefore, the children could be adopted right away. This was definitely an option for us. One negative for us, but not for everyone, was our feeling that we were shopping for a child. We could look at thousands of pictures and read thousands of stories about each child. We didn't count this idea out altogether, but we did set it aside as our top priority until we had completed more research. But we did go back to the agency that works with children in foster care and does local adoptions.

We scheduled a meeting with a case manager, Kim. We flooded her with questions, which she answered, clarifying the details. Kim explained that waiting for a child who is given up for adoption can be a long process. Accepting a child into our home from foster care could be particularly difficult. The child might not stay in our home because the court could send the child home to his or her biological parents. We asked how often this happens. Kim stated that she didn't have a specific percentage, and there were no predetermined factors that would ensure we would be able to adopt. This was very scary. What if we fell in love with our baby, as I was sure we would, and the court sent him or her back home? Would this be something we could handle? Kim explained that this was something we would have time to think about. She explained that there is a process to become a foster/adoptive parent. This process includes classes, home inspections, references, and so on. Basically, she gave us a checklist. We decided to start the home study process, which did not lock us into a commitment to a specific child.

The home study process included a twelve-week class, several home visits by Kim, first-aid training, adding extra fire extinguishers and smoke detectors in our home, and setting up a room for a child within the age range we had chosen. We decided on birth to twelve months as that age. With a child of this age, we would have the most time with our child as possible. We also had to provide a list of disabilities we were willing to accept and care for. We were not well educated in the long list of choices, so we marked that we would accept any child within the age range. Kim explained that we might have to wait some time before an infant came into foster care. Paul and I had resolved ourselves to accept the fact that the child who was meant to be with us would arrive on the date and time he or she was supposed to. There was no way we were going to pray for a baby within six months or whenever. This would be like praying for a child to be hurt. We received our license to care for children from foster care, and the wait began.

Our preparation for months of waiting was cut very short when we received a call the very next day about a baby girl. We were so surprised that we were being asked to have a two-week-old baby girl placed in our home. This was our first go-round, so Kim told us to listen very carefully before making a decision. I was thinking there wasn't anything that would make me say no. This is what we had wanted for such a long time. Kim told us to sit down. Reluctantly, we did. She said there are never any guarantees, but there was a good chance this child would never go back to her biological parents. We asked why. She explained that they were arrested for injury to a child. The evidence against them was very strong. I asked what injuries the baby girl had. Kim said the baby's name was Savannah and she had been shaken. "What? What does that mean?" we wondered aloud. Kim explained that Savannah was currently at the children's hospital and needed caregivers who would visit her daily as if she were their very own. She might be in the hospital for a while, as the extent of her injuries had not been determined yet. We had another question: "If we say yes today, are we locked into adoption even if we determine this is more than we can manage long-term?"

Kim said, "If you are willing to be her loving person while she is in the hospital, prior to her discharge we will have a conversation as to whether or not you want to accept her into your home." Kim said the doctors and nurses would be informed of our role in Savannah's life, and information regarding her condition would be shared with us. She explained that we would be able to ask all the questions we had so that we were very clear on her needs and prognosis.

Kim's final statement brought me to a definite *yes*. "Babies in NICU have better outcomes when they have a loving person by their sides," she said. Even if we were not able to be her forever family, we could love her for the moment. We went straight to the hospital to see our little Savannah.

When we arrived at the hospital, Kim was there. She had made arrangements to have the head nurse sit with us before we went in to see Savannah. She would prepare us for what we were walking into. The nurse, Pammy, who would prove to be our biggest supporter, shared that Savannah had been shaken. She explained that infants' brains are not fully developed. There is room in the skull for growth. She also explained their neck muscles are very weak, and their heads are heavy and disproportionate in size to their bodies. She went on to say that shaken baby syndrome is when a baby is shaken violently. Generally this is done in anger in an attempt to get a baby to stop crying. When a baby is shaken violently, his or her brain basically bounces around inside his or her skull. Pammy then explained that Savannah had suffered a lot of injuries. She was on a respirator to help her breathe, she had a cast on her leg from additional injuries, and she was swaddled to help with her broken ribs. Furthermore, her eyes had hemorrhaged severely; they were bandaged to guard against additional injury that could result from any light.

Then Pammy stopped and looked at Kim. Afterward, she gave us an out: "If this is too much, the entire hospital staff will understand if you leave." I had to ask my next question just to verify Kim's statement: "Do infants have better outcomes when they have a loving person with them?"

Pammy said, "There is no explanation for it, but it has proven true for as long as I have worked in the NICU." That is all we needed. We asked to see our foster daughter. We may have said foster daughter, but in my heart I already knew I would never leave her as long as she needed me.

The next six months seemed to go by so quickly. I took a leave of absence from work and visited my Savannah every day. I would sit and talk to her; read books; gently touch her hands; and gingerly lay my hand next to her small, broken body. Paul would come to the hospital every chance he had. Savannah's broken bones healed quickly, as Pammy had explained they would. She was able to breathe on her own after about three months. The bandages were removed for tests and treatments, but new ones were put back on each time.

We arrived at the hospital together to celebrate Savannah's seven-month birthday and were informed she would be ready for discharge soon. We would need to discuss with Kim our plans for the future. If we were going to continue to care for Savannah, we would have some training to attend. Paul and I looked at each other for a split second and at the same time said, "When do the classes start?" We would be taking our daughter home as soon as she was ready and as soon as we knew how to care for her.

We were trained in physical therapy. Savannah would have regular therapy appointments, but practicing her physical therapy exercises at home was vital for her continued progress. We were trained in occupational therapy, which would also be practiced at home, as would speech therapy. We were going to be a very busy family. Our days became a very well structured routine of attending appointments and practicing each of her therapies. The therapies became games in our house, accompanied by storytelling. We were not expecting miracles, but we knew she would make more progress than any doctor could have ever predicated.

Savannah celebrated her first birthday today. This is a huge milestone for many babies, but more so for our little one, who could have been shaken to death, literally, when she was just two weeks old. We received a call from Kim in the middle of our little party. She informed us that the criminal case was completed today, and both parents had been sentenced. Before I could think, I said, "Well, I hope their sentence is as severe as Savannah's life sentence as a result of all her injuries."

Kim said with a very apologetic voice, "They each got two years of state jail, a $5000 fine, and a felony on their record." Kim explained they couldn't prove either parent "knowingly" injured Savannah, which meant that they could not be charged with a third-degree felony.

I started to cry. What kind of justice is that? The $10,000 combined fine wouldn't even cover her medical bills, and our Savannah would be disabled for life. This was not justice. How could her parents say that they didn't know? Aren't parents educated before they leave the hospital with a new baby about not shaking their baby? Kim explained that the education of the parents was not documented in the hospital record.

I took a deep breath and said, "Well, at least they can't get her back, since they will be in jail, right?"

There was a long pause from Kim. After her silence she stated, "CPS will still have to go back to court in the family court of law in order to terminate their rights." This court date wasn't for another four months.

All I could think to say was: "Well, I guess children don't have rights like dogs do. Serious injury to an animal, including tripping a horse is a third-degree felony. I love animals, but there is something wrong with this picture when a child's injuries mean less than those of a dog, cat, or horse."

I stopped my venting and told Kim I had to let her go because I had something so much more important than focusing on two evil people. I had a beautiful little girl who had presents to open and birthday cake to play with. Savannah didn't care about the courts, remember the people who hurt her, or worry about any of the unfair laws of our great state and country. Savannah has known love since that day in the hospital and has known it unconditionally.

Savannah turned two years old today. Yes, a whole year has passed. The parents' rights were finally terminated. I was told I really didn't want to know how difficult that fight was. Kim, Savannah's caseworker, has completed the process for her adoption. We are in court today for the last time. We get to legally adopt and keep our little girl, who has been our daughter from the day we got a phone call that she was broken.

The caseworker was asked to testify in court for the adoption. Savannah refused to sit still, which, if you have a two-year-old, you will know is true of most kids this age. But the fact that our two-year-old is not sitting still is a miracle. The judge stated that since we were the only ones in the court room on this very special day, she could roam around.

The judge began to ask question after question. "Didn't you [Kim] tell this court Savannah would never walk, talk, or see?"

Kim looked at our baby girl and then at the judge. With tears in her eyes she stated, "This is what the doctors kept saying, but they obviously have never known the love and dedication of these parents or the fight in this little girl."

Savannah is twelve years old now. She is not a cheerleader, doesn't play sports, isn't head of her class, and isn't obsessed with a cell phone or Facebook. Savannah smiles prettier than anyone else in the world, walks without braces, will talk your ear off if you sit still long enough, and loves books. If her doctors were to describe her, they would say she is legally blind, has a speech impediment, is developmentally delayed, and has debilitating scoliosis.

Her doctors would say that she has long-term injuries as a result of shaken baby syndrome.

Savannah will tell you they are all wrong. She will tell you she can see just fine as long as she doesn't break her glasses. She will tell you she talks just fine if people would just listen better. She will tell you she may not be as smart as some, but she is much smarter than lots. She will tell you her back may not be straight, but it is stronger than people without a backbone. She thinks that cell phones make too much noise and that sitting at a computer all the time is boring. Savannah knows where she started and will tell you the people she started with were not her mom and dad. They were the people who broke her so that Mom and Dad could fix her with their love.

That's *our girl*.

CHAPTER 9
PICK UP A BAG

You have just experienced a handful of stories of the lives of children who entered this world in various cities and states around the country. They started out in different families. They were each exposed to their own forms of child abuse and neglect. Some started their lives like so many of us, with happy families and regular childhood experiences, and these regular childhood experiences were interrupted by a crisis or tragedy in their family, such as the death of a parent. It is scary to think that at any moment, any one of us could have ended up in a family crisis that left our world in shambles. Yet some of these children, unfortunately, were born into a family that only knew abuse and neglect, starting with their parents and maybe even grandparents who were abused as children. This is called a cycle of violence and not always easy to break.

Many parents say that they would never hurt their children. Have you ever sat up late with a screaming baby and for a split second thought that a little smack would shut him or her up? Instead, you placed your baby in his or her bed and walked away. But what if you were past the point of exhaustion and made a different decision?

Have you ever loved someone so much that life without that person would leave you empty and lost? You may say that the loss of the love of your life would not make you neglect your children, but have you been there?

Have you ever had a car accident, medical diagnosis, or other disabling injury that left you in so much pain that medication became a staple in your day just to manage the pain? Have you ever found yourself addicted to drugs when you didn't see your life going that way? Again, you may say that such an event would never come between you and the care of your children. But once again, have you lived with that kind of pain, that kind of addiction?

Families do not start out planning to abuse or neglect their children. Maybe they were raised in a family of abuse and neglect and are simply repeating the cycle with their own children because they don't know anything different. What if every child in foster care who has known abuse and neglect also knew what it was like to be loved? What if every child who has been part of violence had someone to show him or her how to break out of the cycle of violence?

There don't have to be any "what ifs." Every child in foster care is adoptable and worthy of love. It is the people in each and in every child's life who need to do the work, who need to fight the good fight. A child cannot know the love and support of a family if the adults in his or her life merely sit by and push paper from one side of their desks to the other. Being a caseworker or social worker for a child in foster care is not all about going to court, attending meetings, and moving kids from one foster home to another. As a caseworker, you are the biggest part of each child's life. You are his or her first voice. You are the one who needs to go the extra mile and believe that every child on your workload deserves love, deserves a family.

Every court, judge, guardian ad litem, and attorney needs to look at the children, not just the "case files" that cross their desks.

They need to realize that these are lives of children that they are making decisions about. The law may say that biological parents have "rights," but those in power need to remember that every child has a right to not be hit, has the right to not be used as a sexual toy, has the right to not live in fear, and has the right to be loved. It is easy to see how difficult it could be to weigh the rights and needs of two completely different groups of people: the parents and the children. This only means that all decisions should not be looked at with only the adults in mind but also should consider the children who have to rely on the adults.

So you say that you don't work with children in foster care; you're not a caseworker, social worker, or anyone in the courts. Fair enough. This doesn't remove you from the equation. The number of children currently in foster care within the United States is well over 400,540 as of AFCARS's (Adoption and Foster Care Analysis and Reporting System) July 2012 report. Over 104,000 are legally free and waiting to be adopted. Is every family who is looking to have a child a perfect match to adopt a child from foster care? The answer is maybe not. The real question, though, is how would you know if you never look and get to know one of the many children who are looking for and who want a family of their own? I can hear so many of you saying, "I couldn't sit at my computer and shop for a child online." With 104,000 children looking for a family, please share if you know a better way to match families and children. The professionals working with foster children cannot go knocking on every door and introduce children to those who say, "Well, yes, we are considering adoption to grow our family." Websites provide the best avenue for sharing children with families and families with children. Websites like www.childwelfare.gov provide each individual state's listing of children looking for a family. Still don't want to feel like you are shopping for a child? Let the kids and the adults working with them look for you. Families can list themselves with sites like www.adoptuskids.org. This allows the workers who are looking for families to find you. This way, you aren't shopping for a child, but you may experience a longer wait time to find a child.

Maybe you just picked up this book because it looked interesting, you were bored, or a friend recommended it...You do not work with children, and you are not interested in adopting. You can still pick up a bag. Volunteers are needed in every state. You might volunteer in a Big Brother/Big Sister program; donate clothes or school supplies; or provide some service to help locate families, such as a photo shoot for a child or sibling group.

It has never been said that carrying or helping carry someone else's baggage is easy. It is worth taking that extra step. Foster children who find their forever families are more likely to break the cycle of violence when they have children, which equates to fewer children in foster care in the next generation. Foster children who find their forever family are more likely to finish school and even attend college, which equates to less families dependent on welfare. Foster children who find their forever families are more likely to avoid criminal activity, which equates to lower prison populations. Forever families do not produce perfect children, but they sure do make every one of their children's lives more optimistic and give those children a greater chance at success in life.

So now are you ready to pick up a bag?

K. A. Cory is an advocate for children. She has worked in various areas of social service, including child abuse and neglect, for twenty-seven years. That experience includes serving as a caseworker and supervisor at various state agencies serving abused and neglected children.

Cory earned her bachelor of arts degree in social work from MacMurray College in Jacksonville, Illinois. She earned a master's degree in organizational management of social service agencies from the University of Phoenix. Cory has been married to her husband Robert, who retired after twenty-six years of service in the Navy, for twenty-five years. They have three adult children.

www.ingramcontent.com/pod-product-compliance
Lightning Source LLC
Chambersburg PA
CBHW062009280526
45787CB00005B/2031